PRAISE FOR

Maeve in America

"If Tina Fey and David Sedaris had a daughter, she would be Maeve Higgins. (And while I'm building the fantasy family of comedy, let's put Nora Ephron somewhere on the family tree.) Higgins's essays cover subjects ranging from what kind of shelter dog she would be to emigrating from Ireland, but a single thread weaves through each one: that elusive feeling of laughing around a big lump in your throat." —*Glamour*

"Wickedly funny . . . with incisive humor and deep humility . . . Higgins has the rare gift of being able to meaningfully engage with politics and social ills while remaining legitimately funny." —*Publishers Weekly* (starred review)

"Witty, humane, and topical, these essays offer an enlightened perspective on modern American culture while probing the energetic inner life of a bright young Irish comic. A warmly intelligent and insightful collection."
—*Kirkus Reviews*

"If this is your first time reading Maeve Higgins, I'm jealous. She's hilarious, poignant, conversational, and my favorite Irish import since U2. You're in for a treat."
—Phoebe Robinson, *New York Times* bestselling author of *You Can't Touch My Hair*

"Maeve Higgins is hilarious. She is the true Irish voice of our American generation." —Amy Schumer

"Maeve Higgins is brilliant; but her brilliance isn't the braggy, headlight kind that tries to trap her subjects deer-like in a cold, dead glare. Instead, she lights every room she enters with warmth, welcome, and generous rays of sheer funny. And in this book, she illuminates the world."

—John Hodgman, bestselling author of *Vacationland*

"Maeve Higgins is easily one of my favorite, most treasured comedic voices. She is one of those rare artists who makes her unique point of view relatable and refreshing, leaving you feeling like you've been on the same page with her your whole life." —Kristen Schaal

"Until space aliens land in America, Maeve Higgins from Ireland is the next best thing. She offers fresh and insightful perspectives from a faraway place on all we take for granted."

—Neil deGrasse Tyson

"Maeve Higgins is the funniest writer I know. And *Maeve in America* is just so smart and joyful. I especially like it when she's unhappy. Because she's very funny about it. Always be unhappy, Maeve!"

—Jon Ronson, author of *So You've Been Publicly Shamed*

ABOUT THE AUTHOR

MAEVE HIGGINS is an absolute legend, but she's modest about it. The host of the hit podcast *Maeve in America: Immigration IRL*, she is a comedian who has performed all over the world, including in her native Ireland, Edinburgh, Melbourne, and Erbil. Now based in New York, she co-hosts Neil deGrasse Tyson's *StarTalk* on National Geographic and has appeared on Comedy Central's *Inside Amy Schumer* and *@midnight*. Maeve's one true love is writing. She's the author of two essay collections for Hachette UK, and her work appears regularly in *The New York Times* and *The Irish Times*.

Maeve in America

Essays by a Girl
from Somewhere Else

Maeve Higgins

PENGUIN BOOKS

PENGUIN BOOKS

An imprint of Penguin Random House LLC
375 Hudson Street
New York, New York 10014
penguinrandomhouse.com

LIBRARY OF CONGRESS CATALOGING-IN-PUBLICATION DATA
Title: Maeve in America : essays by a girl from somewhere else / Maeve Higgins.
Description: New York, NY : Penguin Books, [2018]
Identifiers: LCCN 2017052944| ISBN 9780143130161 (pbk.) |
ISBN 9781101993651 (ebook)
Subjects: LCSH: Higgins, Maeve. | Comedians—United States—Biography. |
Internet personalities—United States—Biography. | Conduct of
life—Humor. | LCGFT: Essays. | Humor.
Classification: LCC PN2287.H496 A3 2018 | DDC 792.702/8092 [B]—dc23
LC record available at https://lccn.loc.gov/2017052944

Printed in the United States of America
1 3 5 7 9 10 8 6 4 2

Set in Adobe Caslon

For Liam, Aoibhinn, Cathal, Hazel,

Nora, Sadie, and Daniel.

You think I am your aunt,

but really I am your mother.

Contents

Swimming Against Dolphins

SLIPPING INTO SHOCK, using all my strength just to keep my head above the choppy waters of the Pacific Ocean, I couldn't muster up the energy to climb back onboard the boat. I just clung on to the ladder, making a sound quite similar to a shouting goat. The tour guide leaned over the side and called out, "Up you get! Come on, nearly there, you'll be fine!" in a chirpy but anxious tone, the one you'd use to coax an aging relative back into the nursing home. I couldn't move. She climbed down the ladder and hauled me up on deck herself, tiny and all as she was. I lay there for a minute, curled up like a fern. A vomiting fern. "Are you pregnant?" she asked, and I shook my head. "It's just that dolphins are the midwives of the sea and it seemed like they were trying to help you." "No, they weren't," I said, coughing up seawater and my lunch. "They were trying to kill me."

You see, I once swam with wild dolphins off the coast of New Zealand. If I told you that, and nothing else, how would that statement make me sound? Am I a chill girl, a surfer, not just on the waves but on life itself, someone who just goes with the flow, happy wherever, a lithe beauty laughing in the flickering light of a campfire, ankle bracelets glinting, sun-bleached head of hair thrown back? Do I love nature, treasure all the creatures of the sea, and commune with Mother Earth as seamlessly as a sunflower, as fluently as a fish? I would love for that to be the case, but that is absolutely not the case. It's dead wrong. It's purely aspirational, and does not match the truth even a little bit.

Here on dry land, I blunder around the place making mistakes all day long, misunderstanding others, managing to over- and underestimate my own motivations and capabilities as I go about the endlessly tricky business of being a regular human being. So why should I be any different under the sea? Particularly when I'm surrounded by dolphins—the most malevolent creatures known to man.

At that time, I was coming to the end of a three-month stint of comedy festivals throughout Australia and New Zealand. I ask you again, how does that statement make me sound? Like a world traveler, a touring artist, shuttling between airplanes and hotels and theaters with a host of funny and charming friends, taking things global? There is truth to that, of course—I was getting opportunities to work and travel that I had never dreamed of. I mean that. It was never my dream to stay in a hotel in Bundaberg with an older English comic who closed the show every night with a routine, that never failed to bring the house down, comparing his child's birth and wife's body during said birth, as akin to watching his favorite pub burn down. I'd just kind of followed along a string of various successes and failures and found myself here; I was on the road, a job coveted by many, but one I never quite chose. And this was the reality—lots of checking in, to flights and hotels and venues, lots of time spent with people I'd never voluntarily choose to spend time with, and plenty of bewildered, if not hostile, audience members waiting for the big loud boys they preferred.

Please understand, there were occasional bursts of magic too, like the time I saw electric-green frogs hopping around in a thunderstorm outside the theater in Cairns, or the time in Wellington when I felt like the audience and I merged consciousness when I was discussing the merits of pineapple upside-down cake. Perhaps it was one of those gems, some bewitching nugget of connection and magic, that I was hunting for that fateful day I booked myself on a tour to swim with dolphins.

I doubt that, though. I believe that it was something a little more mundane. It was a laziness on my behalf, a reluctance to figure out my own dream, and a tacking on to other peoples' dreams, that made me decide I simply had to swim with dolphins. All my life I've meandered around, wondering what I should do with myself. Aside from getting champagne in your eye, or being snapped at by your pet toucan, bemoaning a lack of purpose is the most privileged problem in the known universe, so I won't drone on about it. Suffice to say that when my friends dreamed of moving to Paris or running the Grand Canyon or having a baby with Jake Gyllenhaal, and set about achieving those dreams by respectively learning French, running, and finding a different brown-haired guy, I peered into my own future and saw only fog. Not having a dream didn't bother me, until someone would ask where I saw myself in five years, or what my dream was, or some such hideous question. And then I'd say, "I'd like to swim with dolphins," and they would mercifully leave me alone.

Now, here I was taking the necessary steps to make this dream that was not mine come true. At seven in the morning I boarded a minibus driven by a blocky, scowling woman. I was the only one on it for the first fifteen minutes but that didn't stop her from using her microphone headset. "Just got one more hotel pickup and we'll be off to Rotorua," she boomed. I asked her how many people were coming. "Just two, because it's off-season now, mate, it's unusual for people to still be hanging around." We stopped and collected a very old American couple. I helped the lady in and her hand was soft and tiny, like a chick. It took the pair ages to get on and settled. The driver rested her head against the steering wheel for a second, then said, "And we're off." In a menacing way. The old lady made a "here we go" face at me and I was very glad she was there.

We exchanged small talk for a minute or two but it was difficult to hear over the amplified sighs of the driver. Also, I reminded myself, this was their holiday and I shouldn't inflict my company-starved self on them too much, so I sat two seats away from them and looked out the window. The driver reeled off information in a bored tone that bounced off the minibus walls. "Quick fact about glowworms for you guys. The fellas that burn the brightest, well, they are the hungriest fellas." In the beginning, I and the Americans encouraged her by saying, "Oh," and nodding at each other, but that seemed to irritate her. We piped down and let her get on with it. Two and a half hours passed in a long, slightly nervous heartbeat.

We got to Rotorua and were deposited underneath a sign with three arrows pointing in different directions, one to THE DOLPHIN EXPERIENCE, one to THE WHALE WATCHING EXPERIENCE and one to THE CAFÉ EXPERI-

ENCE. I never found out what The Café Experience was, but I'd imagine it was a cup of coffee and perhaps a pastry in a mildly comfortable chair. The American lady smiled a goodbye to me, linked her husband's arm, and I watched as they slowly walked in the direction of The Café Experience. I wished I could join them, and take photos of scones and flat whites to show the folks back home. Instead, I waited alone on a low wall, looking out at the restless gray sea. I thought the Pacific was supposed to be a sort of turquoise color that came lapping gently up along white sandy beaches, but not so, at least not there. Annoyed, I threw some stones into the sea, and tried my best not to think about what was rattling around inside there under the water. The thing is, even thinking about fish makes me shiver. I have ichthyophobia, self-diagnosed, and not rational. It started when I was thirteen and my brother's peculiarly athletic goldfish would leap at me from his tank and flop around my room for long minutes as I stood on the bed and screamed for help. The last time I went to an aquarium, in 1999, I fainted. I can't bear to look at fish, and I hoped I wouldn't see any that afternoon.

At noon I went inside, paid my money, and joined the group. There were about twenty people, mainly backpackers from healthy socialist countries like Norway, and a few middle-aged couples with teen children. Hearing them all chatter away happily, I realized that nobody else was a lone comic. We sat and watched a short video about how great dolphins are, and how we should behave around them. As I watched them swim around on-screen, I shuddered involuntarily. It showed them speeding along, slicing through the water like bullets, but giant fish-shaped bullets. I started to get knots in my stomach. Until that moment, I hadn't thought about how much dolphins look like very big fish. They are mammals but they look like fish, in the same way tomatoes are fruit but look like vegetables. It began to dawn on me that I, a person who is terrified of fish, should probably not swim with dolphins.

I shook the feeling off. I would be fine! I reminded myself that dolphins are not fish, fish are mackerel and pike and . . . and goldfish. People love swimming with dolphins, it is a well-known dream, the ultimate bucket list item to be ticked off, a dying wish. Many people travel long distances and pay huge amounts of money to achieve this dream! Besides, it'd be crazy to turn back now, after the video and the safety talk and everything. These dolphin guys were charming and warm-blooded, not a million miles away, evolutionarily speaking, from Michael Fassbender.

By all accounts, they were very sweet creatures. The voice-over said that dolphins empathize deeply with humans. Apparently, they even adopt peoples' emotions as their own sometimes, and when depressed people swim with them, the next day the dolphins wake up with a "oh, what's the point anyway?" feeling. Upon hearing this, a couple of English girls crinkled up their faces and said, "Awwwww," and their father squeezed his wife's shoulders as they shared a look. Fortunately, continued the narrator, the dolphins we were going to hang out with were wild and therefore not overly exposed to human sadness, so they had a great attitude.

A woman wearing a dolphin experience T-shirt and flip-flops came and introduced herself as Kate, our dolphin guide. She opened with a warning. "I want to let you all know that there's a very real possibility we may not actually see any dolphins." My panic, which had been rising steadily since I saw a dolphin on-screen, began to subside. Kate explained that since the dolphins were wild and the area they roamed around was the actual ocean, the boat's captain didn't know where they were all the time. "If we can't find them using our sonar and radar machines, you'll get your money back, and in that case at least you'll have had a nice boat trip." I began to clap, but quickly stopped when nobody else joined in. I smiled through the rest of her speech. There was an out! The dolphins just needed to keep to themselves and us humans could all relax and have a cup of tea.

After loosing another couple of unnerving facts on the group—"Dolphins can see behind them" and "Dolphins have sharp, conical teeth"—Kate sent us off to change into wet suits. The English sisters shrieked and laughed at each other about how unflattering the wet suits were. Changing into a wet suit is definitely more fun with a group of friends. I found myself in that awkward position of doing an amusing thing with a group of people I didn't know, but who all knew each other. I kind of laughed along aimlessly to show I was fun and relaxed and recognized the humor in situations, and that I certainly wasn't some kind of dangerous drifter who studied human behavior so she could mimic it and pass as one of them, no, no, not at all.

With much difficulty, I zipped up the back of my rubbery onesie and waddled with the rest of the group to the pier. We boarded a wide, flat, dolphin-seeking catamaran. It was drizzling now, and the sea looked like she wanted to be alone. Kate, however, was full of optimism. As she handed out binoculars, she told us to shout if we saw any movement at all. We traveled far, far out to sea. The farther we got from land, the more I questioned my reasoning. Why was I doing something I did not want to do? It was never my dream to be a touring comic, or to swim with dolphins. Why was I following this path that someone else had tramped down ahead of me, and what did I think I was doing, rushing to keep up with them and stay ahead of the person coming behind me? It was getting really cold, and my teeth began to chatter.

As the waves swelled, Kate shouted to us that we were in a reliable part of the sea now, and the boat was going to zip around to the dolphins' favorite locations. I squinted at her. It's not like there are libraries or Mexican restaurants under the sea, so I wondered why they'd prefer one spot over another. I didn't ask; instead I pretended to look through the binoculars.

I immediately saw a huge school of dolphins breaking through the waves on my side of the boat. I felt a rush of pure terror. I put down my binoculars wordlessly and began to plot a way of distracting a boatload of people from seeing the one thing they were longing to see. No such luck. My face betrayed me, that's what always happens. My face is so expressive that my sisters can tell what flavor ice cream I'm thinking about at any given moment. One of the English girls looked at me, then straight out to where the dolphins were. She screeched. I cursed her.

The boat followed the dolphins and we all took up positions along the back deck, ready to jump at the sound of the horn. Suddenly the water was alive with them, all around us. Everyone was giddy with excitement but I absolutely did not want to jump into that gray water with its big, irregular waves. I was furious at myself for being so scared. So what if this wasn't my dream? I'd gotten this far doing what I thought I should, hadn't I? This was a once-in-a-lifetime chance, I was on the other side of the world, I was a grown woman in a wet suit, and besides, dolphins were just mammals.

I instructed myself to jump in with such authority that I did, immediately. I jumped before the boat had stopped or the horn had gone off. My first thought was that the water felt like a thousand stabbing knives; my second thought was, *SHARK!* I thought I saw a shark under the water: the fin, the flank, the flat eye on the side of the horrific head, taking me in. I was not thinking straight. There were no sharks. I couldn't get a grip on what was happening, but I knew panicking was not the answer. Not realizing I was underwater this whole time, I tried to calm myself by taking deep breaths, but they quickly turned into large gulps of seawater. I managed to surface, getting my head above water just in time to see the boat disappear and realize I'd jumped too soon.

A wave tucked me under the quilt of the sea again and I saw through stinging eyes that the creatures I was surrounded by were not sharks, but dolphins. They were standing up casually, smiling at me. Apart from the freezing cold and the intense fear, here were two things I hadn't anticipated. That the dolphins would be vertical under the water, and that they would laugh as they tried to kill me.

A standing dolphin leveled itself and swam toward me, fast. It swirled under my legs and I felt its firm fish body. Underwater, nobody hears you scream. Then they all rushed at me, brushing off my sides and turning me over, swishing past my hands as I tried to paddle. I kicked and spluttered and tried to remember how to swim. I totally could not breathe. I remember thinking how unfair it was that these dolphins were going to drown me, but everyone would think it was an accident. People would say, "What a beautiful way to go, she left this Earth guided by the angels of the ocean." They may even etch a couple of dolphins on my gravestone, what horror!

In what I assumed to be my final moments, there was no Super 8 reel of beautiful moments flickering through my mind. I didn't remember my dad going around the table and covering our small heads with his big hands and kissing us on the forehead, or my cat Edie's slow blinks, or a brilliant boyfriend reading out loud to me one warm city morning. I simply thought again and again, *These psycho fish are going to drown me and get away with it.*

At the last possible second, I remembered that, back at the presentation, Kate had told us that if we got into trouble to put one fist straight up in the air. "Just do the Black Power salute, and the boat will come and pick you up." As the dolphins continued to ram me and giggle, I used one arm to hold up the other, and struggled between waves to keep it up. I hoped that, while I couldn't see them, surely someone on the boat would see me. *Those morons all have binoculars*, I thought, fully blaming these strangers for my own stupidity, for my own failure to be the master of my own destiny, the captain of my own ship.

Thankfully, those sweet morons did spot me, and I heard the boat approaching. The dolphins, predictably, fled the scene. That's when Kate hauled me onto the boat and asked me if I was pregnant. After she'd sluiced the vomit off the deck I lay there wrapped in a towel, face turned away from the happy adventurers who were paddling close to the boat and actively trying to lure the dolphins into any form of physical contact. I stayed there, lying on the deck and shivering, repeatedly counting the row of brightly colored life vests stacked under the seat, as we sailed back to Rotorua.

With the clarity lent to me by a recently emptied stomach and a blanked-out, restarted brain, I understood that I had to figure out what I wanted to do before I drowned doing something I thought I should do. Back on dry land, I got shakily onto the waiting minibus. My eyes were burning from the salt water, my hair was matted, and, understandably, I smelled terrible. Despite this, I sat one seat closer to the Americans. The wife peered over the seat through her huge bifocal glasses and asked, "How was your dolphin experience, little one?"

"Great, thanks!" I said, and started to cry.

Rent the Runway

THE MOST PERFECT FILM in the world is called *Now, Voyager* and I hope for your sake that you've seen it. It's a Bette Davis film from 1942 about a frumpy spinster who has a nervous breakdown, then gets therapy, loses weight, and plucks her eyebrows, thereby transforming herself into an elegant, independent woman. Bette Davis leaves the sanatorium and goes on a Caribbean cruise, and that is how she meets a charming architect, played by Davis's greatest leading man, Paul Henreid, a married man who is traveling alone.

In a fantastically revealing scene, Bette Davis has borrowed her glamorous cousin's wardrobe for the cruise, and shows up to meet Paul Henreid in the cocktail lounge of the ship. She looks incredible in a gorgeous white gown and an evening cape decorated with sparkling beaded butterflies. Paul Henreid is knocked out, as he should be. They sit and he sees a little note pinned to her back—it's a reminder from Bette Davis's cousin about just how and where to wear the cape. He laughs a little, and says something sweet about how birds can borrow feathers and still be beautiful. Instead of laughing along with him, poor old Bette Davis is humiliated. She spirals into an irretrievable funk and runs off to her cabin, tearfully calling out, "This should pigeonhole me for you, all right. They don't suit me at all. In fact, they're perfectly ridiculous. You're quite right someone is playing a joke on me, although it's far funnier than you realize!"

Nobody was actually playing a joke on her. It just felt that way when her carefully constructed and still-brittle persona took a small knock and completely crumbled. I think about this scene occasionally, when I can feel myself changing but am not quite there yet. It's a painful time, straining to reach a version of myself I've dreamed up, with only the old version of me to help get there, the one who is determined not to be left behind. And, of course, the scene shows how deceptive appearances can be. I was reminded of *Now, Voyager*, of a woman unsure of herself on the inside but looking absolutely fine on the outside, the last time I wore a borrowed gown. You see, I went to a ball. I did, you know! And I too was a beautiful bird wearing someone else's feathers. The ball was a fund-raiser for the Irish Arts Center, a sweet and important little cultural center way over on Eleventh Avenue in Manhattan, with a black-box theater space full of seats rescued from a movie theater in the 1980s. It looks like a narrow three-story house and has a makeshift charm about it. I often perform in the theater space downstairs while upstairs people learn to speak Gaelic and play the fiddle. I adore it there, but also look forward to the fancy new building they are raising funds for.

As I totted up my expenses in preparation for the ball, I realized I should probably be fund-raising for my own renovation, because my funds were the lowest they'd been since I worked in a skateboard shop and gotten paid in T-shirts. I'm bad with money, but money is worse with me. Some days it pours in on top of me and I have to fling it away to be able to breathe. Other days I look for it everywhere and there is none to be found. I'm embarrassed about my relationship with money, and I often read violent articles online with headlines like "Take control of your $$$ now, ya dumb bitch!" But I can never seem to do what they tell me. My actual fortune keeps changing; as an adult I've been so rich I bought a car for cash and never used it, and I've been so broke I've brought my coins to a check-cashing place on Church Avenue and tried to convince the woman working there to give me a full dollar instead of eighty-eight cents. Money feels like a tide that comes in and out, controlled by a moon I can't reach. One time I said that to a bank adviser in a Chase branch in East Harlem, and he looked at me like I was crazy, but then he canceled the fee I'd incurred for being overdrawn, so I think we all know who won that round.

The ball rolled around during a month when the tide of money was very far out, and I could not afford to buy a dress. If I gathered all the cockles and mussels left clinging to the shoreline, I could just about afford to rent a dress. There is this wonderful place called Rent the Runway, where, Cinderella-like, I could borrow a dress for a fee, and unlike poor Cinderella, I didn't have to give it back at midnight. I had the whole next day to lounge around in it too.

I felt totally fine about renting a dress, although I promised myself I wouldn't tell anyone I had done so. I resolved to just say thank you if anybody complimented me, as opposed to explaining in too much detail just why they were wrong to do so. In the past, I've ruined many a generous utterance by breaking it down and explaining where the lie is. "Oh, this old sweater? Please. I got it from a thrift store and I'm quite sure this here is a bullet hole, it smelled like blood and sulfur when I bought it, believe me, but it was only seven dollars!" Not this time.

This time, I would be a successful adult who happened to choose this dress from a selection of many that hung in her walk-in wardrobe in a separate room from her bedroom that definitely wasn't a fifty-minute subway ride to Manhattan and definitely didn't have a salmon-colored sink in it that was left over from when her apartment was a dentist's office. I would wear the dress with a casual air, maybe even a nonchalance that suggested to onlookers I was a little bit tired of going to balls all the time, but compassionate enough to support the cause.

As is the anxious person's way, I did a lot of research online before deciding on Rent the Runway. I was charmed by their website, particularly the review section, where customers give a short biography at the top, listing their size, shape, height, and age, as well as other outfits they've rented and how they felt about them. I love these reviews, and the fact that they are often accompanied by photos that were taken on the night, or right before they headed out for the evening, full-length candid shots they snapped in their bedroom mirrors. My favorites are action shots—seeing the girl at her friend's wedding with her date's arm slung around her shoulders, or on a dance floor screaming along to the track being played, surrounded by her girlfriends, who all share that wild look of new mothers on the loose.

Hanging out on the review pages of Rent the Runway is like being part of the biggest and chattiest changing room in the world. I liked the sisterly tone and the safety that comes in an all-femme place online. I spent some time investigating a black sequined romper from the Robert Rodriguez collection. A romper is a top and shorts all together in one piece, like a baby would wear, except black and covered in sequins. One reviewer stated, *I wore this outfit to the Beyoncé concert in LA at the Staples Center. All eyes were on me.* I doubt that the concert-goers turned their backs on Beyoncé—whom they had bought tickets to see, and who is, after all, Beyoncé—craning to better gaze upon this vision swaying in the audience behind them, resplendent in her temporary sequins. That said, the reviews were unanimously positive, despite repeated mentions of the garment's tendency to "ride up" and warnings not to dance with your arms above your head, as that would cause a wedgie. The idea of wearing a pre-worn and pre-wedged romper did not appeal to me. Besides, I knew that nobody, not even a princess who was also a baby, could get away with wearing a romper to a ball.

I paid a visit to the brick-and-mortar Rent the Runway store, located in the middle of the Meatpacking District, a concrete space full of gowns you can try on and feel against your skin and lift your arms and inspect your butt in. From the outside, the store looks like an upscale boutique, with designer gowns in the window and elegant employees in black wafting around inside.

It's only when you're inside the store and wandering among those dresses, lifting them up and pulling them out, that you notice that they are all a little big or slightly too worn or just a tiny bit used-looking, and that's when the entire place suddenly feels like the dress-up box at a theater workshop.

I was overwhelmed by choices, and hurriedly pulled out a few cocktail dresses to try on. They were mostly black, mostly shaped like the dresses a doll would wear in the 1950s, the type of dress that's absolutely perfect to wear to your grandson's bar mitzvah. I'm not used to dressing up; my professional life doesn't allow it. Writers wear grubby, misshapen outfits that eventually mold to their hunched-over bodies, and stand-up comedians are the same, except with an added parka jacket, because they are forced to leave their house for shows. There in the store, surrounded by pretty dresses, that bold woman in my head who envisioned herself in a romper had fled, leaving me floundering. I timidly chose the plainest dresses, the ones least likely to trip me up, until a swan of a girl with blond hair extensions on her little head and a measuring tape around her slender neck came gliding across the floor to my hapless self, offering assistance. I nodded at the creature, in wonder and agreement.

Ten minutes later, I found myself in front of a trio of mirrors, spinning around and clapping, actually clapping my hands together, as half a dozen women in various states of undress collectively cooed at how stunning I was. The swan had zipped me into a strapless fishtail dress, oyster-colored; a dress that sounds like hell, but looked like heaven. Honestly, I couldn't get over myself. Was it really me? Could it be true that I was this elegant Grecian statue, animated now through some sartorial spell with the sole purpose of devastating men and inspiring women? I was light-headed at the prospect of entering the world in this powerful form. Or perhaps I was just dizzy from all the twirling.

I floated on up to the cash register to secure my future happiness. A different swan, older and sophisticated, smiled at me as she secured the dress in its special case. I blushed in anticipation of it all, the way my butt looked in the dress, the snipped-in waist highlighting my abstention from carbohydrates for the past six weeks, and the thrill of stepping into an actual ball looking like a sexy goddamn Cinderella. Then the magic stopped. The dress cost $320. Not to buy, you understand. Three hundred and twenty dollars to rent for a couple of days, after which these swan fairy godmothers would disappear, forsaking me as I turned back into a scullery maid.

The rental cost was determined by the retail price and this dress was a Vera Wang number, expensive and unforgettable. I'd heard the name before, but until that moment of unrequited longing, until that impossible dream of a dress had her exquisite fingers around my throat, I'd failed to understand its meaning. I'd been Wanged. I was willing to be Wanged, even wishing to be Wanged, but I just couldn't do it. I don't mean that I couldn't bring myself to pay that much money for a one-night stand with a dress. I mean I couldn't pay for it. I tried all of my credit cards and they were rejected one by one. I frantically scanned my phone for Venmo accounts and online bank statements, but that did me no good, for any waves of money were long gone and there I was, stranded on the rocky shore. The women waiting to pay for their dresses in the line that formed behind me were quiet and respectful throughout the process, unusual in a city of hurry-uppers, but they had seen me in the dress. They understood. I stepped aside, pitifully putting my cards back into my wallet as the older swan motioned to the younger one to unpack the dress, since, after all, she was no longer going to the ball.

I was going, though, I had committed to it. I felt like throwing a fit, the way Bette Davis did when her new persona was exposed as a fraud. I wanted to run to my cabin, and scream at the other customers about how this was all a joke played on me, a thirty-three-year-old woman who looks like she's made it, but can't even afford a rented dress! Oh, who did I think I was? Sure, I had a two-bedroom apartment in a fancy part of town, but every month was a race to pay for it. Yes, I'd left a small town in a small country and come to the big city to see my name in lights, but here I was, shielding my eyes from those very lights! "That should pigeonhole me, all right," I said, Bette Davis–style.

I didn't scream at anyone, of course; I simply stood by the counter uselessly until a lesser bird, one of those teenage ones with gawky plumage who you can't quite believe will ever become a swan, led me back to the fitting rooms. There, the light seemed different than before. Harsher, somehow, as were the faces of the other people in the changing room, now that I wasn't wearing my oyster-colored super-shell. With a heavy heart I hauled on some of my initial options, the black ones, and settled on a peplum affair with a gold damask design on the bodice. A mourning dress in transition, with a thigh-high slit. Not a bad look—I would go to the ball as a widow trying to get back in the game. Seeing myself in the mirror, stripped of my first choice, I felt a new sensation, a phantom pain, the sort of pain an amputee feels in a limb no longer there. It was just an aftershock of being Wanged, I told myself; it would fade with time. Eyes cast down, I paid up, and left.

The ball was held on the Upper West Side, in a fancy hotel of the old-school variety. Nothing hip about it; instead they had heavy wool carpets and comfortably worn-down banquet halls, a reliably moneyed aesthetic. I'd gotten my makeup done at a Sephora in downtown

Brooklyn, by a woman with hot little hands and a talent for cat's eyeliner. "Even though you got those heavy lids, I can make 'em look wide open, surprised." I blinked at her appreciatively, using all my energy to lift those dead-weight lids of mine. I did my hair myself, straightening the curls, then making them into largely successful waves held in place by enough hair spray to hold a litter of kittens as still as statues for a day. Ideally I would have taken a car to the hotel, one of those low, purring cars driven by a rapper who's more on the business side now. There was no such opportunity—my carriage was the Q train to the C train, at rush hour, so I wore my hoody and rolled my dress up in its plastic shroud, slipping it into my backpack with my shoes. I looked like one of those doll heads that hairdressers practice on, balanced atop a body dressed for a nap.

I changed clothes in a bathroom cubicle at the hotel. The mercifully solid oak doors hid my shuffling from foot to foot as I stood on the sneakers I'd worn on the trip, trying not to touch the floor. Even in fancy places you don't want to stand barefoot in the bathroom, because rich people have worms, too. I wiggled into the dress, packed my old clothes up, and slipped out of the cubicle to inspect my put-together self in the mirror. I tried not to think about the Vera Wang dress. It was never mine to begin with. Neither was this one, but it was what I had on and I forced my brain to focus solely on what stood before me. *Compare and despair*, I chanted to myself, *compare and despair*. I looked perfectly okay. The dress was basic, up to the job, if the job was to have a nice time and to blend in well. I worried that the peplum effect was a little too like a deflated jellyfish wrapped around my waist, but I was gloomily sure that nobody would look too closely. I was no mermaid come to live on land, and I was certainly no Cinderella. I wasn't an Ugly Sister either, just a bystander, unnamed in scene, maybe the youngish aunt of one of the girls hoping to catch the Handsome Prince's eye.

I had assumed there would be a cloakroom, but as the old saying goes, to assume is to make an ass out of you and me. In this case not you, just me: the woman who just changed into a floor-length dress in the bathroom and was now standing balefully by the door to the ballroom with a backpack on her otherwise strapless shoulder. I ducked into the room where a drinks reception was well under way and flung my backpack under a tall table draped with a long white tablecloth. I took a glass of cava from a passing waiter's tray and offered it to the Man upstairs, praying that nobody would spot the backpack. Not that there was anything valuable in there, but they might think it was some kind of explosive device. I stood, alone and worried for a moment, which is a great look for any party, but quickly realized that nobody would suspect a terrorist attack on a fund-raising ball for a nonprofit arts center, and that my bag would be fine. I spotted a woman from the arts center and went up and pulled her elbow just as she was about to take a drink. She didn't think it was funny, but I put that down to her not knowing who I was for a moment. She was kind of startled, until she stepped back and realized it was actually me. She said I looked gorgeous and she didn't recognize me at first. Is there any greater compliment than someone thinking you are too gorgeous to be yourself? Not to me! I was thrilled. It only took her a second to click that it was me, though, and I couldn't help picturing her reaction had I been in that oyster-colored Wang number. She probably would have screamed. Or wept, the way children on reality TV shows weep when their mothers emerge from huge cosmetic surgery overhauls and look completely distorted.

We were called for dinner and sat in a dated, glitzy hall at huge round tables. When I sat and arranged the slit in the skirt, my dress looked fine, but these little rolls of underarm fat kept popping out at either side of the bodice. That would never have happened in my real dress, the one that held me just right, the one that felt like a second skin, a skin more comfortable than my own. More than comfortable, I felt luxurious and effortless and gorgeous in it! That must be how rich people feel all the time, extra-comfortable. Now I was shifting position in my chair, trying to sit up straight. I held my shoulders back, but I couldn't keep doing that and still reach for the butter to put on my little rolls while they were still warm. I mean on my actual bread rolls, not those underarm rolls.

The pang of my missing dress echoed through me as I sat there, and I couldn't help noticing the imperfections around me. The waiters in battered white blazers were so old that they snoozed as they stood and strained to hear our orders. My table was wonderful, giddy and friendly and full of young Irish immigrants. There were a couple of boxers' wives whose husbands were training and couldn't come out, and they were in bright, tight dresses and took regular cigarette breaks. There was a former child actor and a humanitarian aid worker, full of stories of their past lives that expanded as the drinks kept flowing. The speeches were tipsy and outrageous and the petits fours were tragically divine.

It was an event I'd be delighted with at any other time, but I couldn't enjoy it that evening because I kept wondering just how different it would all be if I'd shown up in the magical dress. Wouldn't I be the one holding court at the table, regaling everyone with my just-the-right-side-of-gossipy anecdotes? The waiters would stand up straight and the little birds of paradise would surely not flit so easily away for a smoke. I was certain that the Javier Bardem look-alike at the next table would be drawn to this siren before him, and without any trou-

ble I'd surely lure him into the deep blue sea with me.
Not like this, though, no. Not when the tide was out.

It was silly of me to pine for something so elusive as
the fleeting feeling a slip of fabric had given me one afternoon in the Meatpacking District. Why couldn't I
ignore whatever nerve it had pinched? I simply couldn't,
and it flared up at the ball now and made it impossible
to enjoy myself. I was as foolish as Bette Davis, storm-
ing off to her cabin instead of staying and making love
to Paul Henreid all damn night. What did it matter that
we were not rich and elegant, when there was still so
much fun to be had? It was too late now; the ball was
over. Javier Bardem's twin and his friends left first, followed by the people being honored and the humanitarian. I said my goodbyes, wished one of the bright girls
good luck for her husband's upcoming fight, and
crouched under the table to reclaim my backpack, in full
view of a surprised busboy.

I went back to the bathroom to change into my subway clothes. I tugged at the side of the dress, glad, as
always, to unzip. I put my leggings and hoodie back on
and tied my hair in a ponytail. I walked out through the
hotel, and as I passed the reception desk and reached to
push the brass-paneled door I heard my name being absolutely yelled by a number of voices coming from the
front bar. I looked in, and there was my table, reassem-
bled with a few missing pieces, fresh drinks in hand,

smiling at and toasting me and each other. "We decided to have one more, come in and sit down." "Even like this?" I mimed, gesturing to my outfit. "Even like that," said the remaining bright girl, moving over to make room on the deep green sofa. So I did go in and I did sit down, and it felt like we were just getting started.

Pen as Gun

THE SLIVER OF SHARED SPACE between comedy and tragedy is one that fascinates me. "Haha before wah-wah" is my favorite thing to say to giddy children, because it used to drive me crazy when adults said it to me.

Back then I couldn't articulate why, but I know now that I was annoyed because I only wanted to be high on laughter. I did not want to think about the inevitable comedown.

The sway and clack of karma's pendulum bothered me then, and I still have questions. If too much laughing leads to sadness, is the opposite also true? Can you get so sad that you eventually have to laugh? When things get bad, really bad, where does comedy fit in?

The giggle at a funeral, is it real or just a mechanism

to release tension, the way a gassy baby appears to be smiling? Myself and my comedy comrades, is our work an indulgence or a necessary part of the natural order of things?

These remained theoretical questions until February 2016, when I was asked to lead a comedy workshop in Iraq.

My friend Mark asked me to do it, and I immediately said yes. When I met Mark he was in training for his second New York Golden Gloves tournament, and he reminded me of old pictures of the legendary boxer Jack Doyle I'd seen growing up in Cobh, where "the Gorgeous Gael" was born. I adored him at once, especially the rebel streak I spotted early on, which surely came from his Irish parents. I had a million questions for him when he began working for a media company called Yalla that was based in Erbil, about two hundred miles north of Baghdad and fifty miles from Mosul, where ISIS had declared the caliphate back in 2014 and, at that time, still held.

I wanted to know everything about the comedy scene and content creators in Iraq. Yalla's goal, like most platforms around the world, was to create a place online with content that would be so relatable and so great it would spread by itself, it would go viral, and everyone would get the message. In Yalla's case the message, couched in fun makeup tutorials and sports-gone-wrong videos, was that creativity was better than destruction, and ISIS was never the answer to what ails Iraq. Mark's job was to help foster an independent creative sector in Iraq, and he thought that a workshop where a few U.S.-based comics came to meet and work with their Iraqi counterparts would do just that. With the shining example provided to us by the history of U.S. involvement in Iraqi affairs, I knew that nothing could go wrong.

I told my parents I was going to Kurdistan, rightly figuring they would not ask which part. I don't believe the word "Iraq" came up in our conversation. If it had, they might have pointed out that Iraq was a place still haunted by the U.S. invasion over a decade ago and the consequential havoc it wreaked, or perhaps they could have mentioned ISIS, at that time still rampant in various regions, ensuring that violence reigned across much of the country. Erbil was safe, Mark assured me, but I still felt it was better not to get into a whole detailed explanation of regional politics with my family. "But Mammy, you're not listening to me, ISIS are *miles* away and I'll keep my phone on the whole time!"

I sent the word out—I needed a team! *Wow—sounds awesome*, came the reply. *But short notice / too weird / my wife said no.* Finally, just twelve days to go before the workshop, two people did sign up. The first was my friend Joe Randazzo, a TV writer and satirist, one of *The Onion*'s earliest editors. I'd done a few live shows with him, and the first day I met him I'd had a strange feeling his house had burned down once, and I asked him if that was true. He said it was true, his family home had burned down the week he graduated from college. He asked how I'd known that and I told him I didn't know, but I'd just gotten off a plane and sometimes jet lag made me psychic. Since then, he's thought of me as slightly magic, which is always helpful when I ask him for favors. At the time, Joe had two little kids and another on the way. Despite being due to give birth in a few months, his wife actively encouraged him to go. He found that deeply funny and a little unsettling.

The final person to confirm, thereby completing our trio, was a comic by the name of Mo Amer, whom I did not know personally. I'd heard he was very funny, and a lovely guy too. Both turned out to be true. Mo is a seasoned road comic who arrived in Texas as a child with his Palestinian refugee family. He speaks Arabic and English and had done shows in Ramallah for refugees and in Baghdad for American troops. I'd put together a great team, but whatever about that—these guys' names were Mo and Jo! Myself and my MoJo were headed to Iraq, and this pleased me no end.

You know how busying yourself with details like luggage tags and gel manicures can distract you from the bigger questions? That's what happened to me. I had ignored this one big question that snuck up through my security checks and winked at me from my pastel-pink fingernails. I focused on getting a team together and micromanaging their presentations while figuring out what I should wear. A blazer with the cuffs turned up, of course. That is what people who give talks wear. I got two of them, and that took a whole afternoon of trotting into various Banana Republic stores. The question, the one I avoided because it was too big, was something along the lines of this: What if comedy, and creativity, these nebulous things I've devoted all these years to, are, in the grand scheme of things, unhelpful? Or even pointless? I had vague ideas about how creativity was a life raft for me when the waters of my life got choppy, but I was acutely aware that I did not have any experience trying to stay afloat in a country wracked by war and pain.

Being an Irish child in the 1980s, I have memories of news stories about sectarian violence in the terrible days of the Troubles in Northern Ireland, but I grew up in the very south of the peaceful Republic of Ireland and was lucky enough to escape any trauma. Some specific events, like the Omagh bombing or the two policemen getting beaten to death by IRA men after a funeral, those would rock everyone in the country. A heaviness would descend for a few days as the adults talked to each other about what had happened, and went quiet when we asked why, and turned off the news before the images got too graphic. For the most part, though, the lives led on either end of our tiny island were extraordinarily different, something I only realized as an adult after I'd learned about the reality of segregation and patrols and justifiable fear experienced by people the same age as me growing up in Northern Ireland.

I don't know that there's a definitive way to prove a community's taste in comedy has been impacted by their daily experience, but Northern Irish people are certainly known for their dark sense of humor. A Belfast comedy club owner told me about lines stretching down the street in the days after a particularly bad atrocity during the Troubles. He'd talked about it in terms of catharsis and community. *Before your time*, he'd said, and given me two drink vouchers, because I was doing an open spot and that was the payment. That was true, sectarian violence in Northern Ireland was not a story I owned; by dint of luck and geography I'd escaped it all.

In the week leading up to my departure, I set about preparing my presentations. I was worried I'd say the wrong thing, or be too serious or too flip, so I stayed up all night. Otherwise, I reasoned, I would just lie there fretting. I researched my topics. The French artist Louise Bourgeois said in an interview once, "To be an artist is a guarantee to your fellow humans that the wear and tear of living will not let you become a murderer." That was a good place to start. I would open with a short discussion on comedy as memoir, and close with an even shorter discussion on the history and significance of creativity in times of conflict, and how to keep your creativity intact during those times. I hoped that the attendees would have a lot to say on the latter, but just in case, I scoured the Internet and the library for images and texts to back up my argument that creativity did, in fact, matter. I put together some slides and asked my friend Kinan to translate them into Arabic, then I asked my other friend Brian to put them in a cute format on Keynote so I'd seem like a total professional, like someone who was born in a blazer.

On the subway to JFK, I read *Man's Search for Meaning* by Viktor Frankl, about his experience in the Auschwitz camp during World War II. In it, he called humor "another of the soul's weapons in the fight for self-preservation." I checked in, used my boarding pass to mark that page, Instagrammed myself trying to fit a whole cruller into my mouth at the airport Dunkin' Donuts, and boarded the plane. Mo, Joe, and I were meeting at Ataturk Airport in Istanbul, where Mo had access to the first-class lounge and had promised to get us in too, because he's that cool. Having each arrived on different flights, it took a while to find each other, but we managed it, and the three of us settled in to wait for our flight to Iraq. Blessings on blessings, there were millions of tiny cakes and pastries being passed around. The rich businessmen seated all around the banquettes ignored the treats while we scroungy comedians took full advantage.

In between mouthfuls, Joe asked how I knew Mark, the man behind this whole Erbil trip. I told him Mark was a lovely guy, extremely good-looking, and was an amateur boxer and remains in great shape. I'm not sure why I opened with that, and it certainly didn't go down well. "Wait," Mo said, putting down his éclair, "we're going to Iraq 'cos you've got a crush on some dude?" I backtracked, saying no, that's not why we were going, we were going to help people use their creativity to fight ISIS. Besides, I insisted truthfully, "Mark is not even my type, *and* he's married, *and* I really like his wife, *not* that that matters, 'cos I would never!" Joe shook his head. "Oh, you don't like great-looking guys in great shape?" I told him no, I was actually drawn to chubby, slow-moving guys. I showed them some examples on my phone and that seemed to calm us all down.

Later, when our flight was delayed on the runway because of security issues and a man started punching the seat in front of his when the woman in it reclined, Mo and Joe looked at me with something like unease. The man was moved to the back of the plane, and we eventually took off. Later still, at approximately five a.m., as we stood outside a locked hotel with the dreamy Mark banging on the door, explaining that the clerk was probably at prayer, they looked at me again, this time with regret dawning over incredulity.

Once we were checked in, I slept for two hours and woke up before my alarm with the jittery feeling of excitement and slight dread I always have on my first day in a new place. I showered and attempted to blow-dry my hair, but, as with hotel blow-dryers around the world, this one was as faint as a sleeping child's breath. Furious with my damp hair, I stomped down to breakfast, which was a buffet that included cookies, hard sheep's cheese, honey, and nuts. Heaven. The workshop began at ten a.m. Except it didn't because we didn't have the right cable for the projector.

Forty of my Iraqi peers nodded politely as I squinted in the light and apologized in English. We sat in a hotel basement, in a long room with tables in a circle, all facing me. The participants in the workshop were stand-ups, cartoonists, animators, and comedy actors. Some beginners, some comedy veterans, an equal mix of Kurdish and Arabic speakers. Everyone had been given notepads and pens and small bottles of water. I looked around at these faces as they waited to hear what I had to say about the importance of jokes. My translators, MJ and Ayer, waited too. "Hi, everyone, thanks so much for being here. We will start soon, we just have to find the right cable for the projector, thanks so much again, thanks a million." I noticed Ayer darting between groups of people to relay the Kurdish translation, while MJ just stood beside me and translated loudly in Arabic. I asked them both if it would make more sense to divide the room between Arabs and Kurds, thereby getting my first big laugh. Thankfully, they thought I was joking, starting out strong with a controversial political reference, you know, something topical.

My imposter syndrome, which had been bubbling away nicely at the manageable level every woman has, was now at boiling point. Naturally, the big question saw its chance and moved in. No family in Iraq has been left unscathed by the past years of war and horror. But, um, cheer up? Comedy is important? My voice comes out stronger when I'm scared, and I heard it begin, very loudly. Mustafa, a satirical blogger from Baghdad, was taking notes before I even began. He looked up from his notebook and smiled, putting his hand to his heart to say hello and welcome. Reassured, I continued.

I've played some tough crowds in my time as a comic, and this was not one of them. Everyone was sitting up, leaning in, ready to engage. There were four men around my age, cool-looking in tight suits and hipster hairdos. They came from Sulaymaniyah, a small nearby city they later told me was the cultural capital of Kurdistan. Two of them owned an advertising agency there and the other two seemed to be there as just part of their crew, a cross between cheerleaders and hype-men, laughing at their bosses' jokes and taking dozens of photos for social media. As I spoke and they caught the translation, those four ummed and ahhed in what I hoped was resonance. Even if it wasn't, it felt good to speak to a group of people who didn't just sit there silently, who were willing to give me a chance.

My first lecture concerned comedy as memoir and I began by saying I grew up in Ireland, where people are mortified to stand out, but I live in New York, where self-expression is prized and people pontificate on the effects dairy has on their digestive system loudly and at length. Some smiles. The advertising guys seemed to think the digestive system issues were particularly appropriate for one of their party. Things really picked up when I took myself out of the equation and handed it up to the slideshow, with lines from the Northern Irish poet Seamus Heaney's poem "Digging" comparing his pen to a gun. We looked at Hend Amry's tweets that demonstrate the line she crisscrosses so deftly between political engagement and comedy, and I left the tweets on the screen as small discussions took place between the translators and the participants.

It's a difficult task, making words that are funny in one language match up to achieve the same end in another. MJ, a slightly rakish character with an American accent and an easy jokey manner, took his time and I suspect threw in some of his own interpretations of the material. He was well used to translating for visitors, Erbil being the place many Western oil, construction, and media companies did business from. Ayer, the Kurdish interpreter, was serious and focused, coming back to me a lot for clarifications. "When she says 'nugget' I should say maybe 'small bite'?" We watched a subtitled John Mulaney routine where he makes a wider point about violence against women while being the butt of the joke himself. I thanked them for their kind attention, and asked for questions. There were none. Instead, I got a polite round of applause and one of the cartoonists handed me a caricature he'd sketched as I spoke. It was a little too good. "Like a friendly witch," said Joe.

During the break we had these small glasses of hot sweet tea that are always right on time in Iraq. I gravitated toward two of the only other women in the room, who were sitting together and had been smiling and nodding throughout my presentation. The ratio of women to men did not surprise me. Not because of the country we were in, but just because any comedy workshop around the world is bound to attract more men than women. The Hasan sisters were in their early twenties, with four university degrees between them. We talked about our work. I told them I was a writer and also performed stand-up. Upon hearing the latter, they had a common reaction; they said they could never do that, it was too scary. I said it was probably less scary than the trip they'd made to get here to the workshop; they had come two hundred miles from Baghdad. Russel, the younger of the two, told me she was writing a novel. I asked her if it was funny. Maybe, she said, but maybe not. I told her I hoped the workshop would be useful in some way, and she told me why she had come. She said that in Iraq people understand deeply that life can end at any moment and this darkness is a reason to value the light. She said it as simply and elegantly as that. There was no hand wringing, no doubt about it in her mind.

The writer Matthew McNaught, in an incredible essay in *N+1* about Syrians seeking asylum in Europe titled "Fairouz in Exile," learned an Arabic phrase from a man he interviewed named Ahmad: *Alshirr albaliya maa yadhak*—"It's the gravest evil that makes you laugh." Speaking to the Hasan sisters made me realize that I did not need to worry about the relevance of the workshop. Comedy and creativity were important to Russel as a release and a relief. I feel that way too. If I grew up in Iraq, I'd be the one attending the workshop. Art is not exclusively created by and for the lucky ones. Each life is a deep mine of events and emotions that is ours to dig up and use if we wish to. What we find in that mine might feel too heavy to be excavated, or be broken into such tiny pieces they seem worthless, but that doesn't matter.

The trick is to polish those pieces up, to make them shine with the laughter of recognition, of realizing that we are not alone, that we have this common language.

Later in the afternoon, Joe showed how various online platforms can create or change a narrative. He talked about the comedian's duty to punch up, not down, and this idea really resonated, setting off a wide-ranging conversation about the duty of an artist and the very real risks involved when comedy reveals some truth that the powerful have concealed. A Kurdish cartoonist asked what it was safe to joke about, what were the subjects people felt were guaranteed to be inoffensive, and, more importantly, to not land anyone in trouble. We listed them: animals being like people, kids being like adults, foods of our childhood, bossy wives . . . We agreed that jokes about men and women were always funny, and jokes about animals were universal and wouldn't insult anyone. Others felt that everything should be on the table. Here was a bunch of creative people, debating about the role of comedy in politics, going back and forth about the power they could harness to fight back against forces that had captured their neighbors and in some cases their families—and it was exhilarating.

The openness of the dialogue in the room amazed me. Not long ago a joke in Iraq was always told looking over one's shoulder, such was the danger, one that still exists in many places around the world. A joke suspected to be at the expense of Saddam Hussein was enough to have you disappeared. It was like that in Syria still, with the secret service, the Mukhabarat, all around and listening for clues that a person may not be a devoted follower of Bashar al-Assad. There is no distinction made between a throwaway line or a joke that contains an actual kernel of truth, a clue as to where the joker's loyalty may lie, so it's safer never to utter either. The subversive power of comedy is taken seriously by these dictators and the systems that exist to uphold them, and that is a legacy that would take years to undo.

Ali Farzat, a Syrian artist and head of the Arab Cartoonists Association, joined the workshop by Skype. He called from Kuwait where he now lives, having left Syria after being attacked by government forces who smashed his hands and left him for dead. Mark had tried to get him to Erbil but it proved impossible because of visas and paperwork. Still, the call went well, with the Iraqi cartoonists, including some elderly men, huddled around a phone exchanging low, gentle words of encouragement while a young woman, herself a political cartoonist, filmed the scene and wiped tears from her eyes.

The second day we did a lot of practical work. Joe and I made short videos with two groups while Mo worked with the live performers for a show we were doing that night. My sketch, written by Reshan Hemo, a young

Internet sensation who already had 120,000 Instagram followers, involved me asking directions to a restaurant and two different men pointing me in two different directions. I didn't really get the joke, but went along with it, which is fine to do every once in a while. A Kurdish theater group made up of a husband-and-wife team and two colleagues made a short, really funny video about the differences between American toilets and Iraqi toilets. It was crude and hilarious and clownish, relying on a lot of grimaces and misunderstandings about what to do with the traditional water pipe used in place of toilet paper. I was a little surprised, because they were the same group who had earlier called me over to express their disappointment that I had not included more theater references in my presentation, and asked me whether I understood how powerful theater could be.

In the afternoon we had an hour-long showcase where we watched one man's tribute to Charlie Chaplin, and then looked at a slideshow of some brilliant political cartoons created at the workshop that day while the rest of us were filming. There were cartoons mocking the corruption of various powerful figures, men I did not recognize, and cartoons of ISIS soldiers as bleating sheep who didn't know their way around the country. One of the youngest participants was an IDP (internally displaced person) and he was really shy, but explained, haltingly, through MJ, that his entire family were.

trapped in Mosul, but there were some ways they got news of the outside world. One way was by a radio station called Radio Alghad, which means "tomorrow," set up by people like him, exiled from their own homes, a station that took calls made in secret from people still inside the city. The radio hosts sometimes told jokes, he said, to provide a distraction for the people suffering.

The workshop culminated in Erbil's first live comedy show, hosted by Mo in Arabic and English. The first venue got cold feet and decided against having a big gathering of people there for an evening. Mark found another place, a hotel function room, decorated as if for a wedding with silver and blue LED lights around the windows, and a makeshift stage with a muffled microphone. There was a decent turnout of people who worked with Yalla, a few expats, and some bemused folks who'd come to the hotel to watch a football match downstairs and heard the laughing from the room and wandered in to see what was happening. Mo warmed up the crowd with some much-appreciated jokes about Arab mothers and their need to feed, then brought on the Kurdish theater group, who did a long piece titled "Theater of the Oppressed." Things kind of ground to a halt, and the Kurds got annoyed at the audience for talking. I realized I probably hadn't come up with the world's greatest running order.

Ayer, my previously quiet, worried translator, took to

the stage and tried his hand at stand-up. Peering out from beneath his black baseball cap, he performed in English, and made a super-smart analogy between his country and a new car that people keep trying to renovate with old parts. He did well; he was funny. A dapper stand-up with the greatest mustache of all time, Mr. Ako, followed with a cheeky routine about an unsatisfied wife that absolutely killed. The punch line was something about always making sure to press the right button. After the show he bowed to me and asked the translator to apologize for his off-color joke. I told him it was great, that I'd use it myself if I thought I could get away with it back home The following year I clicked LIKE on his Instagram feed often, on pictures of his cute little boys in a lush green garden, eating ice cream, and on pictures of him in his Peshmerga uniform, rifle in hand, waving from a dusty road on his way to the battle to take back Mosul.

A sketch group called "Educated, but . . ." headlined the night with a mime that involved them creeping through the giggling audience. It was a strong closer; the fact that they relied on mime and clowning allowed all of us to appreciate their gags. One of them did not speak throughout, using just his physicality, his height, and his eyes to achieve a Mr. Bean level of brilliance. We were lucky they made it to the show. These sweet clowns were stopped on their way to the venue by an irate policeman who questioned them for having long hair and wispy beards, kind of like you-know-who, those other clowns, the evil ones a half-hour drive away. They had to call Mark to come and vouch for them, to explain that they were on their way to do a spot at a comedy show, and were not about to join ISIS.

I left Erbil and used my stopover in Dubai to visit my brother and his wife, who live there with my niece Nora, aka, their child. She was just one, and I spent all my time desperately trying to make her laugh, because she has the cutest laugh I've ever heard. She's quite a severe critic, though, and only one of my classic characters worked: that was a nameless elderly servant, an Englishman, stooped in deference, insistently asking her permission to kiss her toes. I repeated the bit in the car going to the airport, leaving Dubai, but Nora soon lost interest and fell asleep. I realized I'd been so focused on getting laughs I'd forgotten to ask my brother about his work as a hydrogeologist. "Oliver! Are you finding water in the rocks or whatever?" He shook his head as he always does when his family reveal how ignorant we are about his work. Then he patiently explained that his current job is not finding water, but finding ways to get rid of groundwater caused by massive amounts of irrigation. I clarified, there's too much water being poured into the desert and it has no place to go? Yes, he confirmed. I noted cleverly that this way of life is completely unsustainable.

My brother told me about the Gaia theory that says humans are a pox on the Earth and she is going to fight us off with a great heat. I was quiet then, as I looked at the beautiful pale baby sleeping in her car seat and the "what have we done?" blues started to play in my head. But, comedy!

Sometimes, all you can do is put on your elderly Englishman servant voice to amuse a baby, or tell your brother he needs to find somewhere to put that water, poking him with a crooked finger until he starts to laugh. I know now that there are old hearts in Baghdad that beat with the certainty of change, and young minds in Erbil that whir with silly jokes and smart ideas. A few months after the workshop, a deadly bomb exploded in the Hadi shopping mall on the same street the Hasan sisters lived on, in the Karrada suburb of Baghdad. More than three hundred people were killed, including some of their neighbors and friends. Their Instagram feeds filled up with photos of the victims, of burned-out cars, and of mourning parents. Russel is married now, and Elly works as an anesthesiologist, often volunteering her time at clinics in the underserved parts of the city. They are both still writing. Despite everything, these are artists, choosing to create rather than destroy.

Call Me Maeve

CALL ME MAEVE. Or Merv, or Maid, or Meev, I don't mind. In this country of millions of people and this city of a thousand cultures, not many people know my name, or how to say it. I'm practically anonymous, except for those times in Shake Shack when I have to loudly spell it out for fear of someone else, Masen or Maddy or Mei-Yin, getting ahold of my peanut butter milkshake and fries when that all-important buzzer calls out to its righteous owner.

Maeve is an Irish name meaning "comedy legend with a cute butt." No, it actually means "intoxicating one." It is an unusual name in America. When I introduce myself I have to explain the pronunciation. I tell people, "It sounds like Steve, except instead of a 'st' sound it's a 'm' sound, and instead of an 'eve' it's an 'ave.'" That's a great little conversation-starter for cocktail parties and mother-and-baby Pilates classes. It distracts people from the fact that I'm drinking three cocktails at once and also that I don't have a baby, I just find that class a lot easier.

As a child, I didn't like my name. That's unfortunate because, it being my name and all, I naturally heard it a lot. "Maeve" made me think of a middle-aged woman with wavy hair like seaweed and floaty sage-colored tunics and clogs, with Celtic jewelry and a keen sense of social justice that she keeps meaning to act on. Perhaps a social science teacher, or some kind of writer. Yuck— no, thanks! Reader, it won't surprise you to hear that I'm almost there. Give me fifteen more years and a couple of pairs of clogs to break in and I'll meet you at the protest. I'll be the one taking photos and not knowing any of the chants.

In his letters and birthday cards to me, my grandfather called me "Maeve the Brave" and often added "who's nobody's slave." All he wanted for me was to be bold and free, encouraging my jokes and stories and giving me book recommendations like *Lorna Doone* and *The Brothers Karamazov* before I was fourteen. I was a big, ungainly child and wanted nothing more than to fade into the walls, so his encouragement fell on reluctant, but not completely deaf, ears. I remember it still, though. Today, when I mentor younger women and sense that they are not taking in what I'm saying, I hope that some sliver will linger, one they can use down the line. Now, if that isn't a social science teacher sentiment, I don't know what is.

I always wished for a flower name, like my sisters. You only need to bunch together a few of my six sisters to make up a veritable bouquet of flowers: Lilly, Rosie, Daisy, and darling little Lupin. There's no Lupin, actually; I wish there were. One poisonous little sister would be a boon for the family. Instead, we have these other flowers, and I feel like their names have informed the type of people they are and the lives they lead. Lilly is sensitive and elegant, with a long neck and unblemished pale skin. She is independent and stands out in any room, not needing anyone else. Rosie is beautiful and popular, with a steadiness people respect. She smells wonderful. Daisy is cheerful and sweet, bringing sunshine to any room lucky enough to have her. Then there's me. Maeve. I don't sound like a flower, I sound like a boulder. Or maybe a type of tree, a dead tree. "The great forest of Maeves was decimated by an outbreak of sooty mold in the eighteenth century and never quite recovered."

Maeve also sounds a little like mauve, the color, and I don't like mauve. Mauve is the color of a depressed lilac. The only place I would voluntarily wear mauve to would be my son's wedding to a woman I didn't much like. I would be that passive-aggressive mauve blob in all the photographs, my unsmiling face peeping out from beneath a large off-lavender hat, letting everybody know just how I feel about this debacle, about how my poor boy deserved better.

A friend of mine works as a scriptwriter and told me that the name Maeve is popping up more and more in the indie spec scripts she comes across in L.A. She predicts that my name will become a name that hipster parents call their children "in the next five to seven years." She explained to me that it can be a boy's name too, which I hadn't known. Now I look forward to 2025, to hearing brand-new Maeves of any and no gender, with honeyed limbs and minimal inbuilt guilt, being urged to eat their chia puddings in the utilitarian café of whatever shared workspace I find myself in.

Another unexpected place the name Maeve appears is in the equally fictional universe that is Anthropologie. "Anthropology" is the study of humans, past and present, drawing on and building upon knowledge from the social and biological sciences as well as the humanities and physical sciences to attempt to understand the full complexity of humanity. "Anthropologie" is a beautiful store that sells a lifestyle idea to those humans it has studied and deemed wealthy and aspirational enough to buy it. They sell clothes and home décor and accessories for women. Women who love, love, love to travel but can't because their job keeps them pinned to Manhattan. Women who adore food but don't eat much, women with a powerful career but a carefree sensibility, rich women who regularly say that money is not the most important thing in the world.

This idea of a life that they peddle so well is one I detest and desire in equal parts. I am simultaneously furious and full of longing as I walk around the Anthropologie store in Chelsea Market, waiting to go upstairs to the Google offices for my free lunch with a friend who works there. My eye is drawn to silk blouses in tribal prints. It's a good girl's blouse; a good girl *with a secret tattoo*, but don't worry—it's just a tattoo of a tiny owl!

I finger a chambray dress that cinches in at the waist and falls just right, a dress fit for the heroine of a romantic comedy. She could wear it in that scene at the farmers' market when she drops a little pumpkin on the hero's foot—what a sexy klutz! This $228 skirt covered with miniature French bulldogs surely belongs to me, a true individual who could dreamily lose a whole afternoon in a secondhand bookstore. I mean, come on, my name is written all over these clothes! It is, you know. My name is actually written on the label. The clothes that beguile me and torment me with how close to the aspirational bone they are come from, without exception, the Anthropologie "Maeve" line.

With the amount of market research and chilling data that a gigantic company no doubt compiled before naming their quirkiest clothes Maeve, I have come to accept that my name is synonymous with "kooky." Do I act accordingly? Why don't you tell me? Right after I place a raspberry on each fingertip and giggle down from my unicycle into a Super 8 camera that's permanently trained on me. Not true, but to be fair, I *am* a comedy writer, and I *do* love listening to radio documentaries while I walk through the snowy woods in my duffel coat and mittens, so perhaps I *was* infected with the kooky virus the moment my parents named me. Had I been named Kelly, would I be an accountant with a long bob who does triathlons for fun? If my name were Cindy, would I be a big-hearted waitress with a rescue pit bull and a motorcycle? I just don't know.

I have not met enough of us to confirm my hypothesis that all Maeves are kooky. Strangely, there is a nine-year-old Maeve living in the apartment over mine, and she seems, if not kooky, then downright naughty. I thought it unlikely in a place like New York that my name twin would be one floor above me, but that is what has happened. It's not a sweet little coincidence; rather, it feels like a small punishment for an unknown transgression against the Universe. It's happening right now; upstairs Maeve has upset her sister and is being yelled at by their mother. "Maeve! Why do you have to always do that?" At this point in my life, the disembodied voice of a critical mother is unhelpful. I work from home. Working from home can mean many things. Lengthy studies of Action Bronson videos, hours spent gazing at the patterns on the floor, counting down the hours to my next snack. It also means being alone most of the time, trying to maintain some belief that I'm doing a normal thing and am not a madwoman who is alone most of the time. That delicate equilibrium is often rocked by sudden screams of, "Maeve—what have you done now? Say sorry to *everyone*!"

There are a couple of well-known, now-dead Maeves for me to look up to. Maeve Binchy is probably the most famous Maeve in the world. She wrote best-selling, heartfelt books like *Circle of Friends*, complete with romance and family and great dialogue that never felt unnatural to read. I felt a sadness when she died because she seemed wise and kind and determined to have fun, and her books all had happy endings. Maeve Brennan grew up in Dublin and ended up in New York, writing short, brilliant observational pieces for *The New Yorker* as well as short stories and novels. The map of New York that she drew out of moments that were otherwise unseen, a map of sparkles and horrors in the form of her "Long-Winded Lady" column, is a friend and a guide to me now.

It would be remiss of me not to curtsy as I mention Queen Maeve, the "Warrior Queen" of the West of Ireland, said to have existed sometime between 50 BCE and

50 CE, if in fact she did exist. It's not known if she was even a real person to begin with, or just a complete myth. Here is what we know for sure about that real person, or myth, from the Internet. Queen Maeve was queen of the West of Ireland and she had a Sheryl Sandberg attitude about gender equality and the pay gap. She leaned all the way in. Under the Brehon laws of ancient Ireland women had equality with men: they had the power to raise their own armies, hold their own property, participate in the court system as lawyers and judges, as well as pick their own partners. Marriage was a contract, not a sacrament, and so could last as long or as short as the couple wished. So you could just try it out for the day, and if it was too annoying, you could call it a day, a daylong marriage, with no hard feelings.

Queen Maeve had five husbands over the course of her life, and one of them was a real troublemaker. He was rich, too, and she got mad, she wanted to be at least as rich as him, to get her "man-share." When she found out he had one more bull than she had she started a war to get her own bull. She conducted a cattle raid and she got her bull! She snatched that bull. Total hero. She had many children, including seven sons, all of whom she named Maine. George Foreman, the former heavyweight champion of the world, who named all five of his sons George Edward Foreman, said it was so that they'd have something in common. Queen Maeve did it because a Druid predicted her son Maine would kill one of her enemies, a creep called Conchobar. At the time Maeve didn't have any sons called Maine, so just to be sure she went on to have five and named them all Maine. Eventually, one of the Maines killed Conchobar, which goes to show us two things. The first is that Druids are more useful than we give them credit for, and the second is that four out of five Maines will disappoint their mother. I could do much worse than have my life goals informed by Queen Maeve. I don't mean "learn to speak Spanish and find that perfect risotto rice." I mean she was a staunch character, a feminist who had a lot of sex with young warriors and was buried standing up, facing her enemies.

I love my name now, ever since I changed it to Charise. No, I haven't changed my name to Charise, although that was my dream name as a child, and if I really was brave, if I truly was Maeve the Brave, I probably would change it. Perhaps if I get married I'll change my name, but just my first name. I'll take my husband's first name. Particularly if his name somehow turns out to be Charise. For now, I'm stuck with Maeve, and Maeve is stuck with me. We've stayed together through it all, the missed connections, the embarrassing mix-ups, and the sweet little compliments from strangers that come glinting into our day from time to time, making us feel special for a minute, saying, "Ooooh, pretty name!"

Aliens of
Extraordinary Ability

IN January of 2014, a girl who had left from Cobh in Ireland (formerly known as Queenstown) journeyed across the Atlantic, and skipped rosy-cheeked off an airplane at John F. Kennedy Airport to start her new life. That was me, compensating for my indoor ghost face with too much blush in a shade aspirationally entitled "orgasm." In January of 1892, a girl who had left from Queenstown (now known as Cobh) skipped rosy-cheeked off a boat at Ellis Island to start her new life. That was Annie Moore, flushed with embarrassment at the unexpected fuss being made over her by the officials on the island. She was the first immigrant through the new processing center that opened its doors on January 1 of that year.

I know she was rosy-cheeked, because *The New York*

Times said so, back in the day. I'm only guessing as to the reason. Maybe she wasn't mortified by the attention and the redness was simply caused by the icy wind whipping through the harbor. Maybe she just lit up with the anticipation of seeing her parents for the first time in years and the relief of no longer being her little brothers' sole guardian, as she had been on their voyage. I have no idea. I grew up knowing all about the people who left my hometown, but nothing about what happened next.

I come from Cobh, an island in the mouth of Cork Harbor, the departure point for more than two million Irish people between 1845 and 1945, the last place *Titanic* stopped before it—well, I don't want to ruin the movie. While other children went to amusement parks, our school trips were to replicas of coffin ships, so named because of the high death rate as they transported people to America during the Irish famine. My classmates and I filed into the wooden bowels of a ship to listen to audio of people groaning, and look at wax figures leaning over buckets. So, you see, this whole leaving thing, it's in me.

I first came to America on a P-3 visa, an "Artist or Entertainer Coming to Be Part of a Culturally Unique Program." The Culturally Unique Program I was invited to was the Kansas City Irish Fest. Kansas City is exactly bang in the middle of America and it's not even in Kansas, it's in Missouri. That's one of my go-to facts to tell guys I'm trying to impress. It never works. Often, they already know. More often, they don't find it interesting and are confused as to why I told them.

The festival was a mishmash of Americana and Irishness and Irish-Americanness. With signs on the walls stating guns were not allowed inside the festival grounds, haggis from Scotland for sale at the food trucks, and Appalachian bands fiddling wildly on the big stage, I couldn't fully get a grip on where I fit in. I woke up, jet-lagged, to a thunderous sound coming from the hotel corridors. Unclear about what I was hearing, I blearily poked my head out and watched, amazed, as young American girls in elaborate dresses and huge wigs pounded the carpet in socked feet, practicing for their Irish dance performances later in the day.

The sun beat down outside, and the water in the fountains in the square was dyed green. You know, like the green water that runs throughout Ireland. Extraordinarily friendly residents, volunteering their time at this huge event, told me about their visits back to Ireland, and explained how Irish they were, and how important this festival was to them and their children. These children, red-haired and grinning, were also Irish? Yes, just one more generation removed, making it five generations ago that the family moved there from Leitrim, a stony little county in the Irish midwest with a population that is currently less than a fifth of what it was before the famine, a place that, today, has more sheep than people.

Annie Moore was on my mind during my first few days in the U.S. Her story was told to me by the genealogist Megan Smolenyak Smolenyak. The reason she has two last names is that she took her husband's name. He too was a Smolenyak, but no relation. Anyway, Megan had figured out a key mystery in the Annie Moore story. For almost fifty years, another Annie Moore was thought to be our girl Annie, the first immigrant through Ellis Island. This other Annie Moore had actually been born in Indiana, and moved to Texas, where she married a man descended from the Irish patriot/ heartthrob Daniel O'Connell, the man who had spearheaded Catholic emancipation back in colonized Ireland and was very handsome, in a James Gandolfini kind of way.

That Annie Moore and her star-dusted husband owned a hotel in New Mexico and all was well, until he died and a few years later, on a trip back to Texas, Annie was hit by a streetcar and died too. It was that Annie Moore's story that caught on, probably because it's such a classic American tale, full of dreams and going west and social mobility. She was held up as a brave little immigrant, who worked hard, snatched herself a good life, and died in an appropriately dramatic fashion. Her descendants were honored in a ceremony at Ellis Island before Megan Smolenyak Smolenyak discovered that she was, in fact, the wrong Annie.

The right Annie, the seventeen-year-old who left from Cobh, never went west. She lived her whole life in America just a couple of miles away from Ellis Island, on the Lower East Side. The tenement home she arrived to on her first trip, her entire family sharing a couple of rooms in a noisy, overcrowded building, was the complete opposite of what I experienced, alone in my oversized hotel bed ordering room service, with plump white pillows and soft woolen blankets to cozy up in as the air-conditioning chilled the huge room around me.

In Kansas City, surrounded by Irish-Americans, I felt like I had met them before, but where? Because of my hometown's history of emigration, every summer the promenade and cafés would fill up with American tourists, arriving by liner into the harbor or by the busload from Cork city. They were usually elderly, and as children we regarded them with a fond sort of mockery. Occasionally they would ask for photos with us, particularly of my freckled friends. They bought soda bread and Aran sweaters, anything that was for sale, really. We joked that you could sell them stones, if you convinced them that the stones were Irish enough. Some American tourists would break away from their guided tours and go driving around the island. They sometimes came knocking on our door, asking to look inside the house, thinking it was a replica of where their ancestors may have lived. Perhaps they were right: we lived in a pretty, old farmhouse, with a half door wreathed in honeysuckle, that would have looked the same one hundred years before. My mother was polite to them, but didn't usually let them in, saying to us at dinner that "those poor Yanks were demented."

The thought that, generations later, their descendants might return to the harbor town they had departed from would surely have amazed Annie and the millions who left with her. People only ever left, and perhaps it was a shadow of that amazement that darkened our feelings toward these perfectly lovely Americans. As a child I certainly couldn't fathom why they would bother to visit a boring seaside town in a tiny nation, sitting on hot buses for hours as they wound their way around the countryside, taking photos of some plain old fields full of cows. America was so cool! Their ancestors had left Ireland for a reason, and now they were reaping the rewards. I didn't know what they thought they were missing. In America, they had Michael Jackson and pizza and money, so much money! Not like Ireland, where the only music we made sounded like sad mermaids singing and I had to share a pork chop with my sister and nobody had any money.

As an adult, when I witnessed this little city in the middle of America drop everything for two days and piece together a version of an Ireland that doesn't exist anymore, I suddenly understood the impulse. I felt sorry then for not being kinder to the visiting Americans, for sighing on the inside when someone told me in a loud American accent they were Irish too. In Kansas City, I began to empathize with those "poor demented Yanks" a lot more. Whoever it was of theirs that left Ireland all those years ago took with them a snapshot of the country, its people, and its culture. The details on that picture faded throughout the years, and it could never update itself to show the changes in the country it portrayed. That picture's opaque story was all they had to go on, except perhaps some Aran sweaters and soda bread handed to them by bemused Irish people a century on down the road.

The place where their ancestors landed was at best a blank slate; at worst, an active genocide site. In their new country, America, they did not have a culture stretching back hundreds of years. There was no set of memories to explain who they were and how they got to be that way; no music, no stories, no jokes, except those that came with them across the Atlantic. Of course they clung to the trappings of a culture they'd left behind, and who am I to begrudge them a bit of corned beef, a stick of salty Irish butter? That's probably just the kind of thing Annie would have felt homesick for. Family lore says her coffin was too wide to fit down the narrow stairs of her tenement house, and had to be hoisted out the window.

It's easy not to think about these questions of Irishness and Irish-Americanness, until something big comes along that forces you to. The first year I lived here, I covered the Saint Patrick's Day parade for *The Irish Times*. Not the big parade, not the one where thousands march and millions watch, the biggest annual parade in the city and the only one that uniformed firefighters and police are allowed to participate in. Not the one that banned gay people from marching under their own banner up until 2015. Not the Fifth Avenue parade, the one that shuts midtown down and marches past visiting dignitaries who sit in front of St. Patrick's Cathedral, led by ranks of white men in black suits and sashes.

Instead I went to Queens, to see about their Saint Patrick's Day parade. A couple of weeks before the event I went to see how preparations were going, and found myself in a small kitchen two blocks away from the last stop on the Q train—it smelled like caramel and clean laundry. I sat chatting with the owner, Tom Moulton, a full-time pediatric hematologist oncologist and part-time baker. He was making soda bread, scones, ginger snaps, and oatmeal cookies. *That old soda bread again*, I thought, *what would we do without it?* Everything he made was for a bake sale to raise funds for St. Pat's for All—a parade founded by Tom's husband, Brendan Fay, then in its fifteenth year. The title explains it: it's a parade for everyone, for anyone who wants to join in.

Every Saturday morning in the months leading up to the parade, Fay and his committee meet in Molly Blooms, an Irish bar in Sunnyside, to organize portable toilets and pipe bands. They even send a truck to Brooklyn to collect puppets from a warehouse there. The puppets are free to use because they have been retired or rejected by theaters, so the committee takes them and distributes them to neighborhood kids who've come along to watch the parade and suddenly find themselves a part of it. I mean, rescue puppets? It's almost too adorable to be true.

It is true, and there are more than two thousand witnesses each year, the people lining the route from Sunnyside to Woodside. St. Pat's for All was founded many acrimonious years after the 1992 ban on gay people marching under a banner at the Fifth Avenue parade. This ban seemed off to me, for many reasons. The first is the fact that parades are the gayest way to travel and should therefore never exclude gay people. And also, it showed how out of step the Irish-Americans behind the parade were with the country they claimed to represent. While they clung to their "traditional values" and fought to exclude gay people from their parade right up through the courts, Ireland itself moved on. In 2015, Ireland voted by a huge majority to legalize same-sex marriage, becoming the first country in the world to do so by popular vote. The big parade, the one that goes up Fifth Avenue, seems solemn and self-important and symbolizes to me the difference between the idea of Irishness and the reality of Irishness. *We're straight, we're white, and the men know best!* versus *We're all different and that's fine, but we agree on one thing—we're not English.*

Last Thanksgiving, I went for a wander around Annie's old neighborhood, and peeked into St. Mary's Church on Grand Street, the one that had been rebuilt after it had been burned down by anti-Catholic nativists in the 1830s. It was self-defense against this kind of violence and bigotry that led to the Ancient Order of Hibernians forming in the first place, and so I see that it started off out of necessity, and with valor. I had this romantic idea that when the Irish first started coming in droves to America, fleeing oppression and famine, they would surely feel an affinity with the people being oppressed in their new country. That's not the way it panned out. By the time Annie arrived, the Irish had a much surer footing in the city's political and social life than the generations before her. They were clannish, looking out for their own; perhaps they had to be.

I have mixed feelings about this. I'm glad that they made it, but sorry they often stood on the backs of other marginalized communities to do so. Annie and her family did not have an easy life here, living as they did in the tenements. But at least they had a network, hard won by the immigrants who came before them, people who looked out for each other and made their new life a little easier. The favor of hospitality extended to her is not extended to everyone, even today. It's troubling to see how privilege accumulates over generations, particularly white privilege in the U.S., and, when people reach a certain level of safety, to see how they pull the ladder up after themselves.

The difference between the Irish in Ireland and the Irish in America has always existed. I love reading accounts of the time the great abolitionist Frederick Douglass visited Ireland in 1845. He spent four months traveling around the country and was a huge hit, appearing to a crowd of over a thousand people in Dublin one day alongside the aforementioned emancipator/dreamboat Daniel O'Connell. The men were kindred spirits with a lot in common: both determined to resist their oppressors, both renowned orators, and both leaders in the worldwide fight for social justice.

O'Connell went as far as calling Douglass "the Black O'Connell," a nickname that must invoke a healthy dose of side-eye in us all. First of all, Irish Catholics suffered hugely under the English, but their situation was not on par with slavery. In a fascinating paper by Lee Jenkins titled "Beyond the Pale: Frederick Douglass in Cork" published in *The Irish Review*, the writer notes the following. "The Belfast *Banner of Ulster*, 9 December 1845, reports Douglass's feeling that Irish people did not always 'sufficiently distinguish between certain forms of oppression and slavery.' The *Cork Examiner* reports Douglass's insistence that 'I stand before you . . . a slave. A slave not in the ordinary sense of the term, but in its real and intrinsic meaning.'" That truth, and the clarity with which it was spoken, are important to hold onto today too, as the American alt-right continues to cultivate the lie of white slavery. Secondly, on the whole "Douglass is the Black O'Connell" thing, imagine deciding that someone is so wonderful that you simply must bestow upon them your highest honor: reducing them to one facet of their identity and comparing them to yourself. Try it! I did, and Jake Gyllenhaal, aka "the Male Higgins," was thrilled and flattered.

But back to what would become the biggest annual event in Irish America's calendar. When the very first Saint Patrick's Day parade happened in 1762, I was but four years old. It sounds like it was a fun event. There were just a few Irish soldiers serving in the British army, and they realized that here in America they were permitted to wear green, and sing songs in Irish, and generally have a good time doing stuff they weren't allowed to do back home, so they paraded around for a while, playing the pipes. In later years, the aforementioned Ancient Order of Hibernians took over the running, and to this day they lead the parade, albeit now under a different name. Those were the people I tried to talk to, and that's how I discovered that trying to talk to an ancient order of anything is tough. Reaching the Fifth Avenue parade committee was tricky, but someone finally answered the phone. They were having a function to honor their grand marshal, so I phoned their office to ask if I could go along to write about it. A voice replied, "Absolutely not."

Having been shut down by the big parade, I took comfort in an invitation to the St. Pat's for All celebration of their two grand marshals. It was hosted at home by the Irish consul general and a chubby black Labrador whose name I didn't catch. One of that year's grand marshals, Tom Duane, looked like a clean-shaven Santa, and chuckled like him too. He was elected to the state senate in 1998 and became the senate's first openly gay and first openly HIV-positive member. Proud of his heritage—all four grandparents were Irish immigrants to America—Duane was arrested many times for protesting at the Fifth Avenue parade. He was among the first politicians to support Fay's parade. It was fun to meet him at a time when the tide was turning firmly in his favor. "Now they're all at it!" he said, a grin ruining the credibility of his attempted eye-roll.

The other grand marshal was Terry McGovern, a softly spoken human rights lawyer with copper-colored hair. In a short speech she honored her mother, who was killed at the World Trade Center on September 11, saying that her mother was the first person to introduce her to the concept of human rights. Then a man pulled out his violin; he looked like an extra from *The Sopranos*, but he played like an angel, specifically an angel from Sligo. He closed his eyes as the notes of the reel whirled and slipped through the assembled crowd and we whooped and tapped, the city glittering beneath us. This right here was a version of an Irish America I felt at home in. Annie Moore had married a German man, and, while she stayed close to her family throughout her life, she lived in one of the most multiethnic neighborhoods in the country. I wondered how she defined her identity, if she ever had time to consider it. Annie certainly never had the option to return to Ireland, so, like many an immigrant to this day, she had to figure out ways to make the U.S. feel like home.

I'm very lucky to get that chance to feel at home here, and even luckier to go back and forth freely between the two countries. For most people around the world, America is a fortress. Forget about moving here; for huge swaths of the global population it is impossible even to visit. Visas to the U.S. are, as a gym instructor once said when I tried to do a burpee, "extremely challenging and likely not possible." I'm not even on an immigrant visa: I'm on a non-immigrant visa, which is still very difficult to get. Before my P-3 visa expired I applied for an O-1 visa, which is, by design, only available to the privileged few. To secure it you have to already be a celebrated individual, or at least have the means to make it seem that way.

There's an O-1A, for individuals with an extraordinary ability in the sciences, education, business, or athletics. Nobel Prize winners, Olympians, Fields medalists—these are the ones who come through on the O-1A. The O-1B is for individuals with an extraordinary ability in the arts or extraordinary achievement in the motion picture or television industry; and that's me! Having been on a TV prank show in Ireland and winning an award for it, I can honestly claim that I have an extraordinary ability in the arts. That wasn't the only thing I needed. As part of my application, I also had to collect testimonials from recognized experts in my field. Testimonials are garnered by asking people to vouch for you, in writing, to the Department of Homeland Security. Not just anybody; they must be supremely successful and way above you on the show business scale of one (me) to a thousand (Diana Ross).

These testimonials are known as "the Twelve Letters," and gathering them is a mortifying process for anyone remotely insecure about their worth as a person and an artist. You may run into some psychic trouble if you are, say, a woman, or an Irish person, or a person who was raised Catholic. Immigration lawyers come up with sample letters, and these letters are brimful of hyperbole. They have to be, to convince the officer in charge of your case that you are indeed an alien of extraordinary ability. Words like "magnificent," "peerless," and "transcendent" are encouraged. My advice to anyone collecting these is to consider taking regular doses of cocaine throughout the process; this will give you the false confidence necessary. If you're not comfortable with that, you will need at least a shot of testosterone in the mornings for the two to three weeks it takes to finish the application.

My extraordinary ability is doing stand-up comedy, carrying out prizewinning pranks, and persuading friends who do voice-overs in cartoons to write letters to the U.S. Citizenship and Immigration Services, telling them what an absolute legend I am. There are scientists in India and filmmakers in Colombia and orphans in Jordanian refugee camps, all trying to get to America, and I'm on my second O-1B visa, which will last me for three more years, after which I can apply for an extension. The question "Why me, and why not them?" has no satisfactory answer.

Annie Moore, that first immigrant through the gates of Ellis Island, never had any papers. She did not have a passport or a visa, and white immigrants did not need them back then. Chinese people were not so fortunate, having largely been banned from immigrating to America ten years earlier. Annie was an undocumented, unaccompanied minor, and she sailed right in. She was greeted with fanfare by the U.S. authorities, who gave her a gold coin to commemorate the occasion, then she was allowed to go and meet her parents, wholeheartedly encouraged to establish herself as a new American.

I think about Annie and me, both of us existing in the exact right set of circumstances to allow our lives in America to happen. We arrived at just the right time with the right qualifications. In her case she was young and healthy and white. Same here, with the addition of a favored career and good connections. I think about the people who were simply born in America, who just arrived on this planet in this coveted little corner, who have never had to consider leaving. I think too about the people who die trying to get here, like my producer Erika's uncle, who suffocated in a container on a ship when he was just twenty years old, the eldest son of eighteen children, the one who was supposed to send for the others in Colombia once he'd made a life for himself here. And I can't fathom what it must be like for the people who have lived here since childhood, who are American in every way save their papers, but have no claim on the place, no path to citizenship. I mean, the sheer dumb luck involved in it all!

There's a heartbreaking part of his autobiography *My*

Bondage and My Freedom where Douglass recounts his time in Ireland and writes about being treated with dignity, treated just like anyone else, really, and what that meant to him as a former enslaved person. "Instead of the bright, blue sky of America, I am covered with the soft, grey fog of the Emerald Isle. I breathe, and lo! The chattel becomes a man." And yet, back home in the U.S., many, though not all, Irish-Americans and their leaders opposed Douglass's fight to end slavery and gain rights for African-Americans.

A book called *How the Irish Became White* is a tough read for those of us harboring any illusions that the Irish struggle for autonomy may have translated to support for black America's struggle for justice. It chronicles the earliest days of Irish immigration, when the newly arrived Irish were in the same social and economic class as the free black Americans of the North. They already competed for jobs, and an end to slavery would heighten that competition. Like most immigrants, the Irish wanted to assimilate as quickly as possible, and soon realized that they had what we now know as white privilege, like in the labor movement where they rose to power, a movement African-Americans were excluded from. It's a tragic and all-too-human story of how one group of oppressed people learned to collaborate in the oppression of another in order to get ahead themselves.

It's also a story rarely told, at least among ourselves.

I've certainly heard a lot more about how hard the Irish had it, about our particular struggle, than about how, despite our own experience and despite consistent pleas from people like Daniel O'Connell back home to support the abolitionists, the Irish largely chose to identify simply as white, not Irish, not immigrant, in this new society where race meant everything. And the Irish definitely did have it rough, fleeing civil unrest and religious persecution, arriving to a new country that was often hostile to them because of their nationality. On Saint Patrick's Day of 2017, with a White House full of Irish-Americans, that was the narrative on blast. Vice President Mike Pence spoke about his hardworking grandfather who left the Irish midlands to make a better life for his family in Chicago in the 1920s, attributing his family's success to grit and spirit, failing to mention that the Irish were always in a better position in America than enslaved Africans and their descendants, freed or not, omitting the part where the Irish at that time leveraged their whiteness to ensure they were better off than Native Americans, and nonwhite immigrants too.

Being white in America is so potent, so seductive, it can blind a person without them knowing it. Being white can make a whole community forget who they are and where they came from. The year Frederick Douglass visited Ireland was the year the country began its terrible spiral into a famine that ultimately killed a million people. There had been food shortages before, and the extent of the disaster was not yet clear, but he writes in a letter of the horror of leaving his house and being confronted with the sight of hungry children begging on the street.

It's painful to look through that lens at the present and see so many powerful Irish-Americans, like Paul Ryan, whose great-great-grandfather survived the famine and fled to America in 1851, doing everything they can to stop today's refugees from entering the very country that gave their family sanctuary when they most needed it. That same Saint Patrick's week that saw a celebration of Irishness in the White House also saw a potato head by the name of Mick Mulvaney, Trump's budget director, with grandparents from Mayo, busily announcing cuts to international famine relief with a shamrock pinned to his suit, unaware of, or perhaps unconcerned with, just how grotesque that was.

What else has happened in the 125 years since Annie Moore arrived? Well, the ban on Chinese immigrants has been lifted, and the ban on Muslim immigrants threatened and attempted, with some measure of "success." Catholic churches are no longer being set alight by nativists, but synagogues and mosques are being vandalized by people on the same tip. In 2012 a Sikh temple in Wisconsin was targeted by a white supremacist who killed six people and wounded four. Nazis are on the streets and hate crimes are on the rise. A man whose own immigrant mother walked through the same Ellis Island doors as Annie campaigned for the presidency by slamming immigrants at every turn, and won. We're hearing echoes so loud they've become the sound of today.

Echoes, of course, are still sounds in their own right. Those sounds never went away for some of us, for black people whose churches have been targeted with sickening consistency from the Civil Rights era right through to today. In 1963, the Ku Klux Klan bombed the 16th Street Baptist Church in Alabama, killing four little girls and injuring twenty-two other people. In 2015, a white supremacist named Dylann Roof hoped to start a "race war" by murdering nine black people in the Emanuel African Methodist Episcopal Church, a two-hundred-year-old church that played an important role in the history of South Carolina throughout slavery, the Civil Rights movement, and the more recent Black Lives Matter movement. I used to think that the early days of immigration to the U.S. happened during a "different time," but hatred unchecked has a way of collapsing time, trapping us all until we deal with it.

I still go home for the holidays. I call Ireland home, but America is my home too. In 2016 I stood on the darkening quayside in Cobh on Christmas Eve, and looked at a statue of Annie there. She is small and capable, her hands lightly resting on her little brothers' shoulders, her eyes gazing back at a country she would never see again. An Irish naval ship had returned to the harbor earlier that week from its mission off the coast of Libya, a mission that rescued fifteen thousand people from the Mediterranean Sea in 2016, though that year was still the deadliest for migrants since World War II, with more than five thousand people drowning as they tried to find safety, or a better life.

On my flight home to New York after Christmas, I imagined meeting Annie today. I'd make a pot of tea and tell her how her family turned out so far. She never made it out of the city, but Megan Smolenyak Smolenyak tracked down her descendants. They are spread across the country: actors and doctors and financial consultants and stay-at-home parents, with Jewish and Latin and Asian blood mixed in with her own. Then I'd explain to her loudly and slowly how to follow me on Instagram, and maybe take a few selfies with that funny koala filter.

Annie Moore never made a fortune, or wrote a book, or invented a computer, and why should she? Why should immigrants be deemed extraordinary in order to deserve a place at the table? She did enough. She was just one woman who lived a short life, a hard one. She had eleven children, but only six made it through to adulthood. Can you even imagine burying five of your children? I can't. I tuck that part away in the "she must have been different from me, with fewer feelings" folder, the delusional one that's full of news stories from faraway places that are too terrible to bear. Annie died before she turned fifty, but she lives on in every girl from a country shot through with rebellion and hunger, and in every immigrant who gives America their humanity, as every immigrant does.

Five Interactions, One Man

Party Tricks

I met Dr. Glasses at a party. It was a low-key house party that I'd gone to with a date, so I was polite about the whole "but who's *that* guy?" thing. The party had a theme, and that theme was apples. I had never come across this before, and was initially hostile. Apples? Why apples? They are so wholesome and outdoorsy. They remind me of childhood treats that are not treats at all. Natural sugar? Get out of my face. Besides, this wasn't a kids' party, and if it was, the kids would surely throw a collective fit when they found out that instead of pirates or fairies as a theme, some Goody Two-shoes parent had chosen apples. And why even a theme? I confronted my friend Dan, the party thrower. "Don't you get it?" he asked, ladling mulled cider into my mug and spiking it with apple brandy. "This is how we get fucked up *and* stay in touch with the changing seasons."

Indeed, I did think about autumn and how nice it was in the park, while my date got fucked up enough for the both of us. I left him in the kitchen, mumbling about climbing trees and how he wished he could do that instead of work. Forever helpful, I suggested he quit his unfulfilling job at the architecture firm and become a forester. "Was he the one in *Training Day*?" he slurred. It wasn't until I was in the grocery store weeks later and saw a man who looked like an ancient Denzel Washington that I realized my drunken date meant Forest Whitaker. There and then, among the laundry detergents, I rolled my eyes all the way up.

Back at the party, I wandered around. Some people were arguing about Israel by the cheese, so I stepped away from that whole situation. I was beginning to think it was a terrible party when I went into the living room and sat next to a bunch of people, including this one cutie who made me laugh a lot by waggling his glasses in fake comedy surprise at something I'd said. Finding me funny and also being funny himself? *What's your ring size, pal?* I didn't ask him that, but I did ask him if he knew what Pilates was. I cannot remember why. He said he did know, and recommended it to patients of his if they had recently had a baby or if they had back problems, but he'd never tried it himself. That's how I discovered that (a) he'd never had a baby, (b) he did not have back problems, and (c) he worked as a doctor. Not only that, he worked as a doctor in an underserved part of the city, which is very impressive and carries a lot of moral, if not actual, capital. I left the party shortly after that, alone, but decided to keep an eye on Dr. Glasses. I emailed Dan in the car home to apologize half-heartedly for leaving my idiot date there and request, with the other half of my heart, all of Dr. Glasses's social media information. Turns out I didn't even have to resort to hounding him online, because the very next week I bumped into him in my local coffee shop.

We Both Love Coffee!

At that time, I lived in Prospect Park South along Church Avenue, and went regularly to a small coffee shop that catered exclusively to gentrifiers like myself. At least, I appeared to be a gentrifier, even though I couldn't possibly have bought a place, let alone rented my own place at that time. In fact, I was paying $700 a month to live in the spare bedroom of a couple's apartment underneath the family who owned it, kind of like a . . . loser? Losers can gentrify too, though, and I much preferred people to think of me as a wealthy white artist who was storming the neighborhood. One morning, on my way to the gym, I stopped in the coffee shop, and there was Dr. Glasses. He was eating a pain au chocolat and was absorbed in the science section of *The New York Times*. Like any clever, absentminded person who is so busy helping others they don't even have time for napkins, he had flakes of pastry in his stubble and melted chocolate on his fingers. He was happy to see me; I could tell because he smiled so hard his cute little chin doubled. We had a giddy exchange where we established that I lived nearby, and once a week he worked nearby, and what are the chances, and oh, doesn't this place have good coffee, and isn't this neighborhood so fun but it's a shame it's changing so quickly, and, what? I'm *obsessed* with Tuesday's science section of *The New York Times* too, and how come it's shrinking, and jeez, well, it was lovely to run into you, and hey, should we swap numbers?

The Least Good We Could Do

Dr. Glasses had a pair of tickets for a Peter Singer talk about his book *The Most Good You Can Do*. The book is all about how to maximize your do-gooding capabilities, like how to earn a ton of money and give it to people who need it, etc. It's a great book. Hearing Singer talk about all these people who look like cold hard capitalists but who are quietly helping people in gigantic ways made me feel hopeful and empowered, which is an ideal set of feelings to have in any prelude to a romantic encounter, don't you think? Afterward we walked around in the balmy evening, looking at menus, deciding where to eat. What a heavenly, underappreciated time that is in any day. The pleasure of choosing, the anticipation of a couple of hours with good food and better flirting.

We settled on a Sicilian pizza place and had a really fun dinner. At one point the waitress tapped her teeth to alert me that I had something in mine. I tipped accordingly, what a great girl. As we wandered to my subway stop, I said, "That was so cool of the waitress to tell me I had something in my teeth. I hate it when people don't." He swore he hadn't noticed, and then he said it was kind of a boring thing to talk about, the etiquette of people telling each other they had something in their teeth. I disagreed. He insisted it was, at the very least, kind of a clichéd thing to say, something that someone always says. "Oh," I said, understanding what he meant. "Yeah, it's like when someone mentions swans and someone else always says swans can break your arm."

He said that he had never heard anyone saying that and he laughed a lot, then we kissed. It was not a good kiss. I know that because the whole time we were kissing I was thinking, *We're kissing now we're kissing now we're kissing now*, and at no point did it feel natural or unselfconscious. Chemistry had fled, leaving physics and biology to cope on their own with these two strangers who had recently eaten pizza pressing their mouths and teeth together and kind of mashing them around.

A Very Painful Rash

After the shabby kiss, we exchanged a couple of texts, but never bothered to meet up again. Weeks later, unrelated, I got an itchy rash under one arm and immediately stopped using deodorant. If you ever need a killer line to open a job interview with, you're absolutely welcome to use that one. The rash spread back across my shoulder blade and became almost unbearably painful. It burned and stung, in a deep way that I felt through my whole chest. I told my friend John, and he diagnosed it, without looking, as shingles. He said he got shingles too, from the stress of being in a nasty relationship. I had no such excuse, so I thought it was because I'd been having too many milkshakes. I went to the doctor, and she said it wasn't unhealthy eating, it was just a virus. She put on a plastic apron, gloves, and a mask as she spoke. By the end of my consultation she looked like a beekeeper, and I had learned that she was about as much use to me as a beekeeper. There's not a lot you can do with shingles, except politely wait for them to leave. And also make sure none of the "liquid from the blisters comes into contact with anyone who has not been vaccinated against chicken pox."

Stuck at home, drifting in and out of pain, having exhausted the listening potential of my friends and family with my not very exciting stories gleaned from podcasts, I grew bored. I got the devil in me, and the devil's sidekick, my phone, was only too pleased to help stir things up. Call it boredom, call it looking for free medical advice, call it shingle and looking to mingle—all I know is I texted Dr. Glasses with my disease news, and he offered to come take a look. I demurred. I did think it was sweet of him to offer, although I think doctors feel like they should offer. In any case, my bedridden self couldn't see any other prospects on the horizon, and decided to ignore the bad kiss and try to give Dr. Glasses another go, once the shingles had moved on.

Eggs for Dinner

I was invited to a dinner party thrown by a new friend of mine, Diane, a performance artist and actor and sort of all-around mystery woman. The idea was that everybody had to invite somebody who worked in a different profession than themselves, thereby creating a big mix of people from all sorts of backgrounds who would not normally meet. Naturally, that didn't work out because most of the people invited only knew people like themselves, but I cleverly used the opportunity to invite Dr. Glasses. We sat around a bountiful table, separated from the people we'd arrived with. Diane, from the head of the table, messily carving a chicken, told us to say a few words about who we are, who we really *are*, and why we do what we do, as in really *do* what we *do*.

I wondered if Dr. Glasses could raise the conversation level above the intense need for self-expression shared by the rest of us, but when his turn came he took up just as much time as everyone else, in an equally charmless and long-winded way. The dinner puttered along, a dancer beside me compulsively swiping her dating app under the table, unable to focus on anything else. Before dessert, Diane explained that she was in the process of harvesting her eggs, and asked that one of us accompany her upstairs to administer her hormone injection. She looked to me, I looked to Dr. Glasses, neither of us said a word. I didn't want to go, but I felt like he should at least offer. Don't doctors feel like they should at least offer? Apparently not.

The seconds ticked by until a harpist seated at the head of the table said, "I'll go." Later in the evening, when complimented for the umpteenth time on his self-less choice of profession, Dr. Glasses revealed something that surprised and disappointed me. He expressed an interest in doing comedy and showed us all a video of one of his comedy sketches. It was very bad. After the dinner, as a group of us stood around discussing transportation options home, Dr. Glasses spotted a bus that worked for him and chased after it, barely saying goodbye. Public transportation in this city is almost shabby enough to excuse this faux pas; it could have been an hour before another bus showed up again. Besides, any hope I was holding out for another kiss, a better one, had flickered almost completely out. But only almost! His darting off was a relief and an insult at the same time.

The Sweetest Coda

At two in the morning, he texted to apologize for running away without a thank-you/goodbye/possibly more. I told him it was fine. Rude, but fine. He said he'd dropped his house keys in his madcap dash, and had to break a window to get into his house. The petals of my pettiness bloomed large and, despite my ambivalence toward him as a potential boyfriend, I couldn't help but feel pleased that this man, this perfectly nice man who had run off instead of staying and falling in love with me, had paid for it in some minor way. I tallied it up in my mean little mind: he wasn't the person I'd imagined, he didn't think I was worth missing a bus for, and I'd been forced to watch a terrible comedy video when I least expected it. At least, I told myself before I fell into a deep, beautiful sleep, at least he'd lost his house keys.

Stormy with the Calm Eyes

AT LINCOLN CENTER ONE NIGHT, some friends and I were loitering around the illuminated fountain, drinking tea out of paper cups and gossiping about which celebrities deserved their careers and which ones didn't, when a cockapoo puppy came bounding toward us, russet curls bouncing, sweet little face shining in the moonlight, eager to make friends. As his dapper owner looked on indulgently, I screamed with happiness, got down on the ground to play with the puppy, and did an entire photo shoot where I pretended he had proposed to me by the fountain's edge. My friend Starlee, the best dog owner I know, stood off to the side, scowling. When the puppy left, after I'd shared the content we'd created together on Instagram, I asked Starlee why she didn't say hello. "That animal was paid for, you know, he was not a rescue." She spat out her words. "That's an Instagram dog." "You don't know that," I replied, defensive, wishing I hadn't tagged the creature's account, which had more followers than my own. I'd forgotten how angry Starlee got when people chose to buy instead of rescue a dog, so I steered the conversation back to pre-puppy times. "Anyway, what about B. J. Novak? All privilege, or some small scrap of talent?"

There are thousands and thousands of purebred animals living their giddy little lives in New York, but the ones that really intrigue me are the rescues. They rule this town. I could live a long, if not exactly happy, life as someone's rescue animal. Rescue animals are prized possessions in New York, and unexpected status symbols. It seems like the older and sicker your animal is, the richer and greater you are. This correlation is quite mystifying to me because if I became crazy-rich and powerful, I would go all-out for proper high-status animals. I would have a panther or an emu, or even one of each, in matching diamanté collars. Ideally I'd have a bevy of magnificent animals that lolloped after me en masse when I took a walk, and waited outside coffee shops while I bought them little treats therein. The barista would know my order, one black coffee for me, and eleven dainty madeleines for the snow leopard and her giant turtle sister. Fancy, wild animals would be a mistake, though, in that I suspect if I did get the biggest and fanciest pets I could afford, people would actually look down on me, and tut-tut at the money I spent while there were free, ugly, and wrecked animals somewhere down the road, waiting for a home. Expensive, designer animals are frowned upon. Instead, people go out of their way to adopt janky, problematic, and elderly animals. They pour love and money into these creatures, sustaining a life that wouldn't last candlelight in other places and times.

This rescue phenomenon is remarkable to me, because I come from a rural background where an animal is supposed to pull its weight. They're not supposed to be ornaments, and certainly not supposed to be burdensome in any way. On a farm, livestock is food, dogs are shepherds, and cats are, however desultory their attempts, mouse controllers. A prized animal is a functional one. But that's back there, and back then. Things are different here in the comfortable urbanity of certain parts of the city where the luckiest ones live out a life of financial rewards and wonderful schools and great coffee. Type A people with great careers and stunning butts eventually swivel their Warby Parkered eyes around to those less fortunate.

No, not always to those *people* less fortunate; I'm talking about those dogs, and sometimes cats, who have fallen on hard times and need a hero. This scenario is the one time in this city when weakness is a plus. Lol-loping Labradors rule the suburbs, but they're far too easy and fun for New Yorkers. In this city, if you're a person or an animal hoping to stand out, I'd advise you to be extraordinarily beautiful. Or else really, really weird. High-maintenance is a good thing; underbites, crossed eyes, and missing limbs are medals of honor for these proud dog owners. Personality flaws and behav-ioral problems are indulgently cared for with therapists and medical professionals employed to their fullest, and everybody wants a feel-good bio for their particular pet. In this "if you can make it here" type of town, it's a pow-erful message not only to make it here for yourself and your family, but to have the time and money to spare to create a whole new life for a helpless creature rejected by everyone else.

And it's become quite the competition. Sometimes I wonder if it is too much for the animals themselves. I meet them, and hear their stories. "Oh, that's Melody, she's actually a cat. She has Feline HIV and two types of cancer, plus she's thirty-two years old and has demen-tia, so you can imagine the amount of meds! Anyway— we had to have three of Melody's legs removed and her remaining one encased in titanium and centered. We call it her 'Prong' sometimes, but I worry that's a bit mean. Her leg cost sixty thousand dollars. Isn't she beautiful?" When her photographer and owner leaves the room to feed the sourdough, I lock eyes with this elderly robo-cat, who then looks beseechingly at the balcony door as if she's begging me to . . . let her go. "But Melody," I whisper, "we're seventeen stories up!" She nods back, slowly, but I don't open the door.

There's an animal shelter across the park from my house. It's a little chaotic, because it's a no-kill shelter. The place is magnificent in that they don't euthanize the animals; even when they're very ill, they try to save them. Then they keep them around until somebody, anybody, shows an interest in taking them home. I visit them often, and there's something I love about the place. There's a feeling of sadness that's redeemed by a slight edge of hysteria and a surviving trace of optimism, like a midtown bar at four a.m. Cats in stacked cages glare out crossly; they don't even try to seem friendly, and I respect them for that. Nobody wants a phony feline. Most of the cats, even the seniors with missing teeth and scraggly coats, get fostered and eventually adopted. The shelter's main focus is on dogs; they have so many dogs! Pit bulls, with their almost goofy, almost scary heads; small silly poodle mixes jumping up and down with anxiety; mongrels with bright clever eyes and great attitudes; and then there is . . . Stormy.

I met Stormy when my friend Jim borrowed him for a walk. You can easily borrow a dog from this shelter— all you need to do is wander in and find a volunteer. The volunteers are often teenagers who would rather not meet another person's eye. I get nostalgic around these teens; it's as if they're from the 1990s, so different from the confident teens of today, with the vocabulary to deal with their mental health and access to wonderful dermatologists. Anyway, you find a volunteer and they get whichever dog needs a walk, no questions asked. You sign your name on a list and leave your email address, and just like that you've got a dog for the afternoon. The email address list seems like an empty formality—there's nothing to stop you from giving a fake email address. Even if you give your real one and you keep the dog, what can they do? Sign you up for Pottery Barn promotions as punishment?

I guess nobody steals the dogs, despite the shelter making it easy to the point of encouraging us to. I had never borrowed a dog for a walk before the day Jim got Stormy, but it was one of those worthy things I talked about a lot and intended to do. I told everyone I know in the neighborhood that they should do it. In fact, I proposed that a whole group of us borrow dogs and have a big get-together in the park on a Saturday evening. "Hey, it'll be like the olden days, as if we are starting a dog-fighting ring!" I said to my friend Emma. She narrowed her eyes in a way I know all too well, a way that says, *Maeve, I know you're joking, but that's a bit much.*

Jim made it happen. He's that kind of person. Very

functional and good. He is a doctor who is constantly trying out new ways of physically improving himself. He experiments with diet and exercise, and all of it works. He looks like the statue of David, if David dressed really sharp and had blond curls cut tight into his beautiful head. Sometimes, when Jim is talking, I get distracted because of the shape his body is making, or the way his elegant brow furrows just enough. Now, listen, I'm not trying to have sex with him, it's not like that. It's more that I enjoy admiring him in the same way I would a cherry blossom tree in May, or a plate of perfectly cooked short ribs. You know? I see him as kind of an object to appreciate. Not sure if there's a word for that. I also treasure his intellect and humor, it's just, you should see his arms. Everybody falls for him. Once, I told him that a woman whose dinner party we'd just gone to had organized the whole thing just to be close to him for an evening, and he demurred. "I'm telling you," I insisted as we waited for our train. "She is obsessed." He pouted. "You're making me feel like one of those secretaries who just gets promoted because she's pretty so she's never sure if she's good at her job!" Meanwhile, two tipsy women sitting across the tracks of the subway platform strained to get a better look at him; one of them even got out of her seat and teetered closer to the edge of the platform, well over the yellow line, squinting to see him more clearly, then nodding back at her friend with her lips pursed like, *Mmmm.*

Jim told me to meet him at the park, so I waited there while he went to the shelter to get a dog for us to walk. He was assigned Stormy. You don't get to choose your dog, and I suspect this affects the quality. It was a busy Saturday, with many families dropping by, eager to find a forever dog. This naturally means that the dogs that have a good chance of being adopted stay at the shelter, showered and ready, making their best come-hither eyes. Stormy was an old boy, a heavy sort of hound. One of his eyes bulged and he panted and drooled constantly, even after sitting in the shade for half an hour. He stood close to my legs, and I petted his coat, which was greasy yet somehow also dry. I couldn't tell if he liked being touched. He just stood, silent except for the heavy breathing and drip-drip-drip of his dribble. Stormy was misnamed; behind his eyes was nothing but a flat calm. Any tempest that had raged within him was long since over. He didn't react to anything, didn't seem happy or sad, or really anywhere in between. Occasionally he pulled on the leash and we followed him, but then he stood stock-still again, so we sat back down to allow him to rest. I wondered if he was depressed, and if I was as dull and irritating to be around when I was depressed. I watched him carefully. Were his nails bitten to the quick, had he put on thirty pounds in two months, was I possibly projecting a little? Stormy didn't flinch at physical contact, but he didn't show any signs of enjoying it either. He radiated ambivalence, and I identified with that on a level I found uncomfortable. *At least I don't do that panting thing*, I thought.

Of course, I felt for Stormy. If he was pretty, someone would fall in love with him. Extraordinarily ugly, and he'd be snatched up by someone who wanted a remarkable dog, or was eager to buoy up their online presence by owning an Instagram personality. If he was ill, someone would see the challenge and the cost and jump right in, what a transformation story! All he needed was a double lung transplant and a face-lift—and look at him now! But Stormy was not particularly anything. He was just . . . there. Barely there. It's usually impossible to have a dog in the city and not get approached by strangers. New York is not known for chattiness, but everyone is united in their adoration of dogs. Businesswomen kneel on the sidewalk to lovingly run a kind finger over an elderly schnauzer's little back, old men do baby voices to a stranger's puppy, and children shyly approach and pet your French bulldog as if he's a magical creature from another land. Which he is: France. But nobody stopped to meet Stormy. At one point a toddler rushed toward us excitedly crying, "Doggy, doggy," and stopped comically close to Stormy, pointing at another dog, a leggy spaniel frolicking in the grass twenty feet away. I wondered if people could even see him, big as he was, our poor old ghost dog. Other dogs, usually so keen to get real close and make a friend, trotted on by without a second sniff.

It was funny at the start. Jim and I riffed about how being an invisible dog could have its advantages, like if Stormy used his lack of powers for good, or at least to meet his own ends. He could spend his days sneaking into butcher shops and spiriting away the best bones, then taking an illicit pee on a NO DOGS ALLOWED sign. Besides, we agreed, not everyone can be the star of the show, the one who lights up a room and dazzles at a dog park. We came to a sort of conclusion that maybe going unnoticed is wonderful, because any creature, dog or person, who flies under the radar is more likely to observe the world as it actually is, without the world bending to them. A low voice, aimed at Jim, boomed, "How the fuck would you know?" and I looked at Stormy, stunned that he could speak, shocked that he would drop the *f*-bomb just like that. Turns out he didn't say it, and neither did I. It was just a thought I had. I want to be the star of the show, the one who lights up a room and dazzles at a dog park. I don't want to be invisible and I don't want this special quiet vantage point. Going unseen is ideal if you're a documentary maker trying to minimize your gaze, but what about a fat teenager, or a middle-aged woman in a wheelchair, or that old man on the park bench opposite me that I only just noticed because he sneezed? Ultimately, being seen is a huge part of life, other people acknowledging our existence is like the sun shining on a little sapling; if those warm beams are missing, the sapling will find it impossible to flourish.

There's this Dustin Hoffman interview I watch online from time to time. It's a straightforward show-business chat where he is discussing his long career and what the various roles he's played have meant to him over the years. When he talks about the film *Tootsie*, where he plays a frustrated actor who has to play a woman to get a job, he starts to get choked up. Hoffman says that he wanted to be as beautiful a woman as possible, but when he watched his own screen test he realized he was not beautiful, and never would be. It's then, all at once, that the value placed on a woman's appearance strikes him. I wonder if he was better off learning the truth in one wrenching moment, a ripping off of the lip wax, as opposed to the way I learn it, a daily tweezing that makes my eyes water still. Maybe the rush of realization was necessary for him, because at that moment he had an epiphany and began to cry. Hoffman felt like the woman he was playing was an interesting woman, and he knew that if he met that woman at a party, he would never have bothered talking to her. He understood then that there were too many interesting women he never experienced knowing in his life, because he had been brainwashed into not seeing them.

Sometimes when I watch the interview I feel deeply sorry for him and all the other men who miss out on whole people, snuffling past them in search of an available doll who really doesn't exist. Other times I feel a great wave of pity for myself, because I have been that interesting woman at a party, and I have felt those eyes see past me. I've experienced those one-sided conversations with a man who had no use for me, I've been there saying clever and funny things, bursting with opinions and ideas that may match or bolster or challenge his own, while being completely aware that he cannot hear a word I am saying.

I should call it what it is: misogyny, that mad rule stating women are contemptible. That is what stuck in poor old Dustin Hoffman's throat, and it sticks in mine too. One summer night in Prospect Park a band was playing on the bandstand and my friends and I were dancing on the grass, dancing quite badly and stopping to chat a lot, as is our way. I noticed my friend Joe, a man who's handsome in a regular sort of way, talking animatedly with a woman who had approached him. I thought to myself that it was quite mean of him to engage with her and lead her on, because I judged by her appearance that he would not be interested in her. These thoughts crowded into my head within seconds, and when I caught them I almost gagged. This learned self-loathing, this misogyny right inside me, felt like a tapeworm creeping up my throat, and I hated it. And, of course, the woman may have been wholly uninterested in Joe, what did I know? The assumption I made, that she was interested, that she had to be, was the very one that drives me crazy when it's made about me. There have been many social situations, from when I was a teenager to the present, in which I've wanted to take a man with a hunted look in his eyes gently by the shoulders and scream at him, "Do not be alarmed, I do not want to sleep with you. I'm just a person, talking."

The sun shone on Jim that morning in the same park, and he appeared to be golden. I looked at him, as he tried in vain to make Stormy drink some water from his canteen. He could be Stormy's savior, the one to bring this dull mess of a creature over to the bright side. What a lovely thought! "It's funny, the contrast between you," I said, though I didn't mean to. "What do you mean, like how we're different species?" he asked, smiling his beautiful, innocent smile. "Kind of." I wasn't quite sure what to say. "I mean, like, physically he's a wreck and you're in such great shape. You know, like, your bodies are just opposites . . ." I trailed off, and in the little silence that followed I smiled in what I hoped was a natural way. I guess my smile could have been interpreted as creepy. Jim's girlfriend certainly shuddered a little, despite the warm day. I beg your pardon, did I forgot to mention she was there this whole time? Anyway, she was, and she said, "C'mon, big guy, let's take you home." I was about to tell her that I was perfectly capable of going home by myself when I realized she was hauling on Stormy's leash, and was more than likely speaking to him, not me. We said our goodbyes. I didn't hug Jim like I usually do. Instead I high-fived them both, which is deeply out of character for me. If you ever see me with one hand raised, please assume I'm signaling danger and alert the authorities. After their awkward departure, I sat back down on the park bench and pulled my baseball cap over my eyes, picturing the rest of their day. They would bring Stormy back to the shelter, where he would blend in with all the other dogs not desirable enough to find a family. Then Jim and his beautiful girlfriend who said very little would go on about their successful, healthy routine of shared newspapers and long runs and familiar snuggles.

Months later, I went back to the shelter on a lonely Sunday to find a dog to walk. I was assigned Amiga, a shy terrier with watchful hazel eyes. She grew more confident when we reached the park, and after tussling with a stick and barking at a skateboarder in his forties she grinned up at me. I returned the grin. I felt like if we went to a party together and someone was mean to me, I could rely on her to immediately get her coat as soon as I said, "Come on—we're leaving." In fact, the longer we stayed in the park and the more squirrels she eyed up, the easier I could picture her being the campy type of bitch who would turn and glare at the rest of the party before we swept out together. I know she would throw her drink at anyone who dared to giggle in the silence. My true Amiga. We stayed in the park for hours, playing around, lying on the grass, sharing water and beef jerky, and then slowly walked back to the shelter. I wasn't upset as I handed her back to the shelter volunteer, who hung his head down so his blue hair covered his eyes. Amiga will be fine. Someone will fall in love with her, and treat her well, and she'll live a long and happy life. I know this because her tongue permanently hangs out of her mouth, and it's ugly-cute in the best possible way.

I looked into the kennels before I left and couldn't see Stormy anywhere. I wanted to see how he was doing, but he wasn't there. Someone had chosen him: that is the only way out of this shelter. I checked with the volunteer, and Stormy had indeed found a home. Blessed day! The person who chose Stormy must not have minded his dry coat, his dull temperament, his heavy breathing. Perhaps today there is some life flickering back into his gauzy eyes, now that someone is beaming sunshine into them. I was wrong about Stormy: I had felt in my bones that he would never be seen, but he was. How unlikely, how lovely! I didn't even mind being wrong. It felt like the time I explained in somber tones to my little nephew that the bouncy castle in their grandparents' garden would be gone in the morning, because the party was over and the bouncy castle man had to take it away that night. Turns out the "bouncy castle man" didn't bother collecting it for two more days. Such a happy mistake I'd made. The baby didn't even question the castle, this sweet rift in the natural order of things, he just jumped on and had another brilliant day, and another.

Compliments Girl on Your Kiss

M<small>Y FRIEND</small> E<small>MMA</small> and I took a car home on one of those hot summer nights when the subway was not running and the MTA had put some shoddy excuse on an official-looking sign that made everybody feel even more furious. T<small>HE</small> F T<small>RAIN</small> <small>ATE DINNER TOO LATE AND ISN'T FEELING GREAT. M<small>EANWHILE PLEASE ENJOY THE DEMISE OF THE INFRA-STRUCTURE OF THIS GREAT NATION BY TAKING A CAR HOME INSTEAD.</small> Emma had played music that night (she is a singer-songwriter), and I was complimenting her work. I had been drinking and I was flowery in my language. *You're putting into words things I didn't even know I felt until I heard them; your work is shimmeringly beautiful and almost decadent in its generosity;* etc., etc. Emma slid down in her seat, almost melting beneath her seat belt, her knees buckling. For a moment I thought she might slip under the driver's seat and disappear for good.

She didn't, instead gripping the edge of the seat as she made a sound of pure pleasure, a trill of being thrilled, that high excited whine made by a dog who really needs to pee when it sees its owner finally appearing with a leash. She squeezed her eyes shut and I kept up my steady stream of compliments. I was kind of joking, but I also meant what I was saying. *I'm calling it right now—your work is exquisite, it's like music with a melody at once familiar and somehow new, it explores the unrelenting divergence of the human condition.* Emma's squeal rose and rose as I spoke, until we both stopped to draw breath and began to laugh our heads off. *I love compliments so much!* she said, almost sadly, before closing her eyes and laying her head back on the headrest.

The perfect compliment is actually contained within the receiver, and to be good at uncovering it you need to shuck the person open like an oyster. Using your mind and your instinct (not a knife) you need to get at their pearl, that part of themselves that started off as an irritant and became beautiful only when they themselves embraced it. My pearl is my weird hair. It is frizzy, curly, and straight all at the same time. Mainly, I resent it and punish it with heat treatments and various flattening techniques, but some days I leave it alone and think it looks . . . totally fine. And on days like that, when I don't tug on it with a ceramic straightening iron or lacquer it down with an expensive potion, instead letting it do its own gravity-defying thing, and someone smiles and says, "I love your hair," I am extra-pleased. Once, when I walked into a greenroom with my hair down, a middle-aged male comic said, "Well, that's competition-winning hair," I thought immediately, *Oh, this guy is wonderful.* There's no such thing as hair competitions, but a compliment doesn't have to be logical to do its job. It just has to identify the pearl and add a little luster, enough to make people feel good for a few seconds.

I love compliments, but can only handle a small amount of them myself. I much prefer to be the one giving them. Like a celiac baker who insists on using gluten, I cannot stand what is in my own product. I physically wince. I trash the compliment I'm offered, and sometimes the person offering it. "This hair? It's like seaweed, and you're mentally deficient if you think otherwise." I can't put my finger on exactly why it bothers me. I'm not cynical about compliment-givers, and don't often suspect ulterior motives on their part. I know that the compliment-giver is more often than not as guileless as a Labrador, the wind whistling clean through their head, unburdened by any nefarious machinations. I trust that they mean what they say, and somehow that makes it worse.

I suspect part of my "no thank you, now put it away" attitude toward compliments is the fear of what would happen if I accepted them. Not being second-rate is scary, because it means you're good to go, there's no more waiting around required. God help the person who pushes compliments at me, because that makes me scared and mean. *Oh, I'm clever and funny and pretty and good, am I? I guess that means I'll have to step up and do a great job at life. How dare you? I am but a wilted flower being blown around by a fickle wind, and I must wait here meekly until death. So keep your compliments for someone who cares, you absolute clown!* Compliments don't jibe with my natural style, which is lamentation and self-pity, so I throw them back like a too-small fish, and while I'm at it I curse the river that sent them my way.

I don't behave like this with anything else nice that's been offered to me. I smile and say thank you. The last time someone made me dinner, it genuinely was not good; it was vegetarian lasagna and it was, as the French say, "Tres disgusting avec too much poivre vert." I ate it, and thanked my host profusely. In fact, I complimented it, saying, "Wow, I had no idea that green peppers even turned that color, it's like witchcraft, but good witchcraft." You see, the fact that they made it and offered it to me negated the fact that the food was bad. Unlike the way I decimate compliments, I would never dream of explaining in steps and stages just how stupid the cook was to make it that way, with those terrible ingredients and that outdated recipe. I did not tell the host my private rules for lasagna, which are, broad strokes, never make vegetarian lasagna, the more detailed version being to fry some pancetta for a moment before you add the beef to the pan. In that case, I mind my manners, so I should know better than to trash a compliment and the person kind enough to give me one. I know the proper response to a compliment, because my therapist told me. "Take a fucking compliment, ya dumb bitch, just say thank you and move it along!" No, wait, my therapist didn't tell me that. Who said that? Oh, yes, the man lying on the ground outside the gates of Prospect Park right after I gave him the finger for catcalling.

The opposite of a compliment is an insult, and if you're good at one, you'll be good at the other. I pride myself on keeping my insult devil tamped down with a little pitchfork held by my compliment angel. I'm very good at giving compliments, and I use my power wisely. I know when a compliment slips over the line to flattery, and I know too when to rein them in. My friend Jon loves compliments so much that I hold back on them when he's around. It's a mean game, I know, but it's truly exquisite to bring him up to the edge, from which he can't help himself from asking, *Did you hear my joke? Did you notice my new glasses? Didn't I do wonderfully back there in the meeting?* I relieve him then: *I loved that joke, it's next-level. Your glasses are cool, like something Lady Gaga would wear. And you did so well in that meeting I was proud to know you, and I think they will definitely feel the same!*

I'm not one of those people who desperately hands out compliments the way an unpopular child hands out invitations to her birthday party. There has to be some self-control employed; if there are too many compliments delivered with too much neediness, they will become impotent, pointless, what's known as "an embarrassment of compliments." Remember the song that went, "Compliments girl on your kiss?" Now, that's a great compliment. Many of us are insecure about our kissing prowess. I've certainly asked myself a number of questions while kissing: *Is my breath okay or can he tell I popped a quick Babybel right before I got here? Should I play dead and pretend he's doing CPR and cough up water like he saved my life? Is it normal for his tongue to bleed so heavily after I'm done with him?* My point is, it's great to get some reassurance.

The problem I have with that song is the line that follows the compliment. "Compliments girl on your kiss. / You're number one girl on my list." Oh, I beg your pardon, you have a list? Revealing the existence of said list does not imply confidence. Besides, the opening lyric of that song is "Compliments to all nice and decent girls, / Coming from the DJ Red Dragon." Oh, dear, DJ Red Dragon. Don't you understand? That does not work. You're spreading yourself too thin. Personalized compliments are the only ones that work. There is no point in complimenting everyone at once. It makes you seem phony and wrong. I've been to too many Irish weddings, the "traditional" ones where women do not speak, when the red-faced best man stands up and says, "Well done to all the bridesmaids, who are all gorgeous today," thereby revealing the true ornamental purpose of women in this sorry affair while also failing to convince any of the bridesmaids that they do, in fact, look gorgeous.

The most memorable compliment I ever received came from a pig farmer's wife when I was twelve years old. My family took just one summer holiday when I was a child, to France, where we stayed in a trailer park and ate lots of bread sticks. We still talk about it, how we spent hours marveling at the canned French food in the supermarket and how my baby sister chewed off the only nipple of her bottle on the ferry there, and my parents couldn't find a replacement and she had to move immediately on to solids, much to her fury. The other summers, we would take occasional day trips, but this was a time before amusement parks and petting zoos, at least in Ireland. We did visit a few pig farms within driving distance, and it was during one of those trips that I got my first future-tense compliment.

These farms were no rural idylls; rather, they were

like pig factories, where the creatures were stacked and stored in crates, frustration gleaming out of their little piggy eyes. They weren't open for tours or anything— my father would just look them up and phone ahead, explaining he had seven kids and one long summer, and ask if we could come take a look. At one farm, right after she'd explained that the sows tend to squash their piglets when they roll over in their sleep and that's why they're separated at night, the farmer's wife turned to me and said, "When you're sixteen, you'll be absolutely stunning." It was an odd thing to say to a twelve-year-old, a chubby one in a BMX sweater, peering at piglets through giant glasses, but it kept me going for years. For four years, to be exact. That compliment withered and died on the vine when my sixteen-year-old self discovered she was pretty much the exact same as all her previous incarnations, and certainly not yet stunning.

That sorry affair did convince me of one lovely thing, though, that is the impact of a compliment can last much longer if the recipient is a compliment squirrel, a creature who stores compliments away and revisits them as needed, perhaps right before she falls asleep, so her chubby cheeks dimple into a small smile at the memory of a kind word, and she dreams of a stunning future. So I will continue to dole out compliments as needed, and I hope you will do the same. As for taking them, I'm working on it. When I see one headed my way, I no longer duck for cover. I catch it softly, like I would a tiny piglet someone had inexplicably thrown to me. I refuse to crate her up; instead, I give her a little kiss and send her out to play in the great green meadow of good manners, where she will thrive and grow into a wonderful old sow who adores herself, oinking praise upon others in between lazily scratching her own back on the fence post and rolling happily in the mud.

Summer Isn't the Same Without You

A S I SQUINTED AND SWEATED to the office on
Monday morning, I realized that summer's here and it's too late to work out. This is the body I find myself in, pale as the moon, heavy as the soil after rainfall, the only one I have to get me through to September. "It's not designed for heat or brightness," I complained to the guy getting coffee beside me in the kitchen. "This is the worst thing about being white and . . ."—I search for the word—"and portly!" He was not white and not portly, and looked at me for a moment before saying, "I believe it, and you should really think about that." I told him it was all I could think about, then I showed him my heat rash.

On summer days, the city boils hotter than the countryside because of the asphalt, concrete, and metal that trap the heat. And all those sizzling hot dogs don't help either, probably. Scientists call Manhattan "an urban heat island," and it feels that way too, shimmering and expanding during the long, sweltering days. Street smells ripen, sidewalks bulge with tree roots, and birdsong turns to bird-roar over the rising pleas of the ice-cream truck. The sun is a mad conductor, whipping his metropolitan orchestra into a din that pummels every sense. Everything gets louder, closer, brighter. Underneath all of this the subway trains rumble along, packed with grumpy commuters, oblivious schoolkids, and anxious tourists, all pressed tightly together. On a stalled 6 train, in a car with a busted air conditioner, a collective sigh goes up. A crammed woman looks up from her phone and asks nobody in particular, "Am I crazy, or is this train taking forever?" A man whose armpit I'm facing and whose toolbox is squashing my feet speaks into my hair. "She needs to chill, bruh." I squeeze my eyes shut and pray silently, to nobody in particular, *Give me an airy mountain, a rocky glen.* The train shunts forward, and only the toolbox keeps me from falling. *Give me a silty stream with moss-covered banks that I may lie down and die in!* I need to chill, bruh.

My bald friend Gary gets to the bar and announces, "This town is so sexy in the summer." I mutter, "No, it's not," as I unpeel the back of my legs from the stool. My friend Lindsay sails in, long-limbed and honey-colored, talking about how she needs this summer to go on for-ever, and how we should go to the rooftop and soak it all in. Gary is happy to, because people wear less up there, and he has his little sun hat with him. I agree to go up on the condition that we sit in the shade, because I haven't plucked in days and the sun loves nothing more than to expose imperfections. The antiseptic qualities of heat and light are much lauded, I know. And bad things fester and mushroom in the dark. It's just that the cold suits me. Put me in a caped woolen coat, see how my gray-blue eyes narrow instinctively against the drizzle, witness my wintry magnificence! Now, wedged into a sundress, I am humiliated.

I watch an elderly woman in a tidy red pantsuit walk-ing her dachshund down Greenwich Ave. Despite the material in their outfits (nylon and fur, respectively), they look cool, unbothered. I examine the woman closely as we wait at a light. Is that . . . talcum powder? She moves away; I'll never know. A cabdriver leans against his car, playing Candy Crush in a blissfully loose shalwar kameez. I look at him jealously. How is it that he can wear so much more fabric than me, yet be so much more comfortable? In the seminal New York City in the summer movie, *Do the Right Thing*, Rosie Perez wears a fantastic yellow tank top. I try one on, but it makes me look sickly. That gives me an idea. Perhaps I could model my summer style on the dying woman in the movie *Beaches*—you know, Bette Midler's dull friend! She wore white shirts with cream cardigans, huge straw hats, and actual blankets. It's settled. I find these outfits ideal, in that they prevent both sunburn and male attention.

Summer makes my battle with body image loom large. I understand that body image, as defined by *Psychology Today*, is the "mental representation one creates, but it may not bear close relation to how others actually see you." I absolutely concede that "body image is subject to all kinds of distortion from internal elements like our emotions, moods, early experience, and much more." I'm sure that my brain is messed up and my body image is refracted through many demented lenses, all of which make it bulge and twist unfairly. Nevertheless, my body image strongly influences how I behave. There are days when I can't stand the sight of myself and prefer to stay in rather than face the world outside in my current form. Isn't that wild? Intellectually, I'm very disappointed with myself. I've let them win! But who is "them"? Isn't it me, deciding what is beautiful and what is important? I suppose I'm talking, really, about thinness. Not being fat. Isn't it crazy to say, "I *am* fat," as if that's the be-all and end-all of me? Fat is just a substance, a type of matter, but it's the matter that matters. If you let it, and I guess I do. I grow furious at myself that I've seemingly subscribed to this narrow set of beliefs that values just one version of beauty. I know too that it's possibly not my fault, perhaps I'm just picking up on what's around me, the space in the world I occupy.

I know I'm sort of beautiful when I'm listening to my friend at dinner relive her breakup and really hearing her, when the sun strikes my eyes at three p.m. and the gold flecks through my iris glint in a way nobody else's do, when I'm absorbed in a game with my nephew. Ultimately I understand that this is real beauty, it's compassion and individuality and connection all at the same time. These are the reasons to love someone. But . . . blah blah blah, you know? I can actually look something like conventionally beautiful—I've forced it from time to time. It's effortful and rare. It takes a village: a trainer, a nutritionist, a makeup artist, a certain angle, the right light, an expression that does not come naturally. I'm very bored by the self-loathing I've felt for the past twenty-five years, and with the help of therapy and books, I've managed to turn down the volume on much of that chatter. But the fact remains that accepting, let alone liking, the way I look has proven elusive.

I resent spending time "working on it," even though I'm one of those hypocrites who likes, loves even, how other women have managed to figure it out. I follow a number of body-positive women on social media, and they're awesome. I don't mean awesome in the way that it's used in the United States, to describe a particularly tasty bowl of soup. I mean awesome in the true sense of the word: jaw-dropping, dumbfounding, epic in scale, and stunning in bravery and brilliance. I thought to ask my friend Karolena, a comedian and plus-sized model, about what body positivity meant to her. The night we'd met she'd said something so funny to me, I've always remembered it. We were both in our mutual friend's indie movie, and I told her that I'd had trouble figuring out what to wear. She'd told me, "When in doubt, boobs out." Then she jiggled, and it was heaven. She was so funny and beautiful and comfortable in her body, I thought she must have always been that way. But even for her, she told me when I asked, loving her body was not an easy journey. She works on it still, and told me that as a black Latina woman, loving her body is a form of resistance, a way of standing up for herself and refusing to feel ashamed of who she is. There are an increasing number of these awesome women—not as many as the hordes of us who stay inside and wish, but still enough to make their presence felt online. I can't believe how cool they are, and I examine them, I share their images, I feel so glad for them, and bewildered as to how I can have so much love for what they are doing, yet count myself out of any such experience.

And now it's summer and there's no swirling coat, no layered woolens, no elegant snood to hide in. It's sticky and humid and ninety degrees outside. Women are wearing tiny tank tops with holes cut out of the sides for ventilation. Skirts are shorter than ever, long legs cross over twice, once at the knee, again at the ankle, like vines in love, and bony brown shoulders shrug off any hint of self-consciousness, while I sweat and fume in my big pale self. I should probably tell you that nobody I have slept with has had any complaints about my body, but that's not the point. The point is that for most of my life I've been furious at my physical form, as uselessly as a mermaid who curses her tail and only wants to be on land. I'm sure if I was unlucky enough to find myself living in a war zone, or with a disability, or even just exhausted from working jobs at three different Star-bucks, body image would be the least of my worries. I tell my therapist about my summer dread. She nods. We've been though this before. Not a solution-oriented person, she proceeds to remind me that she will be away for the month of August. That's going to be the hottest month! What am I supposed to do then? I verbalize in the way she taught me that I feel abandoned (in advance) and this behavior (vacation/disappearing) does not meet my expectations of our relationship. She nods. I follow her eyes to the clock; my time is up.

I go home, and all of this heat and sweat mean I need another shower. Why's this season got to be so confron-tational? I stand still after the shower and look at this body in the mirror, my only permanent companion, for as long as we both shall live, until the second, that same second, when we both shall die. The folds in my belly smile up at me, a big wide smile. I smile back, thinking that this is the truest form of navel-gazing. I cover it, or should that be me, in sunblock and a white dress, then we, or should that be I, head out the door.

I walk alone and slowly through Prospect Park in Brooklyn, the trees leafy and generous, dappling my way. Families are out, every kind of family. Ghanaian teenagers play soccer, old Puerto Rican men dance with their grandbabies, a net is strung between bushes for a volleyball game between a bunch of laughing women in hijab. Various flavors of smoke mingle in the air, and the sun watches over us all, very pleased with himself. I fold the brim of my hat for a second and look up, nodding to my old foe. He stings my eyes and I retreat, settling under an elm tree. It's calm here, the noise of the city just a warm rumble now. Without my body, how could I sit here? The tree trunk is solid as my back relaxes against it, my feet tip outward as my legs give in to the grassy ground. My phone slips out of my hand and I leave it. I don't need anything; I'm not hungry or too full, I'm just here, physically present; for once my brain is lined up with my body and they are both just fine. It's cooler here too, and I can't help but feel that most simple and elusive of feelings: *This is so nice.* Then something tiny and buzzing lands on my leg. Is it stinging or biting? I don't know, but I'm certainly slapping. And just like that, the summer rage blooms within me once more.

On the way home, I get so angry at my body walking up the subway steps I start to laugh. I'm out of shape, and losing my breath a little, my back aches, my face is red. Why can't I skip up those stairs like a little urban deer? Why can't I be one of those small-bodied women who bound around like so many frightened impalas? I picture myself thin and tanned, and grow convinced that everything would be different. I suspect I would be happier, wealthier, more loved, generally better at this and every game. It's so unfair! My friend Mona wants me, her, and our other friend Emma to organize triple dates using dating apps. Emma says we should all dress identically, like nuns, in white turtlenecks with baggy black dresses; that way our dates will have to choose by our personalities only. My problem with this, I explain to them, is that I'm bigger than them. And dressing identically would actually highlight this fact. In that beautiful female way that sees the person before the body, Mona is appalled. *What makes you think that will make any difference?* I explain to her that my experience, and also society, make me think that my size will make a difference.

We're sad about it for a moment. It's so silly, our bodies are on the way out anyway! Daily, they degenerate. It's a long melting march toward old age, with all the brittle bones, saggy skin, and big fat middles that come with it. Even if you're an athlete with a face-lift (yes, Shaq, I'm talking to you), sooner or later you'll end up a wreck. It's the stupidest way to decide who to love, and it embarrasses me constantly to be part of a species that decides who to procreate with based on such a goofy premise. But that is the way things are, at least in New York City in 2018. Mona eventually counters with the classic, "But some cultures don't have those ideas, in fact they're the opposite." Her Iraqi family have at times expressed sympathy that she is not fat. I tell her I'll move to Iraq to find a boyfriend.

Then I remember once more that there *have* been times, in the past, when I've pummeled and starved my body smaller, to the point where my periods stopped for almost a year, and I dipped my low-carb body in wax one hundred times over and sprayed it a sort of orange to resemble a tan. The joke of it all is that I didn't like my body then either. That particular time I was thin is a little foggy, because I was so hungry, but I believe I started to hate my nose. I don't remember why, my poor old nose! All it's done is help, and I've dragged it through some of the stinkiest blocks on the Lower East Side this hot, awful summer. Changing my body made me no more comfortable as I moved through my life and I realized that this problem I had with my body, with myself, it wasn't logical.

There has to be more to it; this violence I feel has to

come from something bigger than this world. There truly is something metaphysical that bothers me about my physical body. Isn't it ludicrous, that I, a person, a soul, a personality, whatever I truly am, am stuck in this body? This body isn't me; if it was, then wouldn't I be more comfortable in it? Surely I'd be like, *Hey, pal, thanks for getting me up these steps*, instead of wishing I could leave it and live my life elsewhere, a simple brain in a jar somehow emitting thoughts and words, or just some code in the digital world, away from the messiness of the physical. Did I even tell you about my bad back? It's bad, believe me, it's the worst. Not only does it contain two slipped discs and the most unpredictable acne known to woman, it also possesses a terrible attitude. Sometimes my back decides to shoot pain down my legs, other times it clenches up in a block of tension and sends messages up to my face, forcing that too to crinkle in discomfort. Most days it's fine, and other bodily concerns crowd in instead. Ostensibly small sensations, sometimes minute discomforts, but they are things I can't elude, because they're on me, or rather they are me. A dry scalp, a sunburn, a cutting bra strap.

On days like that, I want out of my body. Such a liberating idea; I would not lament the time spent squeezing into jeans and blushing at meetings. I'd gladly be rid of reflections in unexpected mirrors that sour my day, and vicious menstrual cramps and sudden mustaches and horrifying photos. *Really*, I decide as I finally make it into my apartment, strip off my too-tight clothes, and dive onto the bed, banging my knee on the bed frame in the process, *I want out! I want out of this body.*

I lie on my bed, eyes screwed shut, completely allergic to myself. A few dizzy moments later, I start to cool off. The mattress holds my back and shoulders steady, my hips and spine loosen and drop, grateful for the support. I notice that the sheets smell lovely, a faint cherry blossom, which I recognize as my body lotion. Without a body, I wouldn't be able to do that lovely thing of putting on lotion after a shower. I would miss the feeling of my father's hand on my forehead when he's saying goodbye to me. I wouldn't get to experience the wide-awake shock of walking into the Atlantic Ocean, and the wonder of my breathing matching up with the breathing of a week-old baby fast asleep in my arms. And what about sex? A digital relationship is fun, an intellectual one thrilling, but the only way to truly know if you've found yourself a real one is to get your two bodies together and follow their orders. I sigh into the pillow, and look down at my body. All the sand dunes, gently breathing in and out, the poor thing is glad to be resting. I don't feel the need to attack her. I know that, without a body, I would not feel what I'm feeling right now, this gorgeous melting into a soft bed in a bedroom golden with afternoon light.

Of course, without a body, I wouldn't feel anything. And that's when my resentment makes a little more sense to me, because, feeling nothing? Now, that's a seductive prospect. Not just to be rid of physical feelings, those odd twinges or slowdowns that make you flash forward to the end, but to be rid of all feelings. With no place to store emotions, how could they sneak up on one the way they do? Imagine not having to feel anything, specifically, not having to feel anything bad! You see, in my extremely tender little heart I'm a tiny baby who longs to live in a paradise where she never has to feel sad or angry, or even mildly unsure about whether she tipped that waitress enough. And when you're a tiny baby determined not to grow up, even good feelings can be difficult. Feelings like love and excitement and joy can hurt, because they are too fleeting or too poignant or just too beautiful to bear easily. Lying there in the golden light of late afternoon, I understand why I so often am loath to be in my body. A body makes me feel everything. A body is what makes me human, a body is what makes me alive. And being human and being alive is difficult. Life flows sweetly at times, but for much of the time it junks and shudders and hurts, so what am I to do?

When life is difficult and painful at times, do I scream for a time-out, or try to step off quietly because, well, it's all a bit much? That little baby in me, the one who thinks she is especially vulnerable because of her self-diagnosed extreme tender heart disorder, she wishes I would. She protests and tries to squirm away, but that baby has to grow up and be stoic for ten minutes, please, at the very least. In the summer, life explodes around us in so many ways it's impossible to forget that *we* are alive. Our bodies are exposed more, so we are exposed more. That's inevitable, that's nature, that's life. I've decided to use my body to help me through, and I will use every part. I must lead with my best foot forward, put my head into the wind, keep my nose to the grindstone and my ear to the ground, and try my best not to bawl my eyes out. I do not see a blissful future for us, a clean and pretty picture of all the senses together in one place, but I do sense a truce coming on between myself and my body, myself and my life. I understand that this has to be, so I accept it. For now, I'm Sisyphus in a sun hat, determined to smile.

Are You My Husband?

I REMEMBER ONE SATURDAY that was filled up with jobs around the house. My brother was chopping wood, my sisters were baking, and I was washing the car. What a cute little team, the seven dwarves to my mother's Snow White! We children always did jobs, it was unquestioned, and my main task was minding the baby. That was a fun job, because the baby in this case was my sister Daisy, who was and is pure sunshine. I was around fourteen then, so she was almost four, and required less looking after than before. I guess that's why I was washing the car. I certainly wasn't happy about it. Lest you think it was a sexy kind of washing, like in that Jessica Simpson music video where she has tiny jean shorts on and is using an extremely large, possibly spermicidal, sponge, I will set you straight.

There was nothing sexy about me washing the car. I had an ancient vacuum cleaner, a yellowed plastic bucket that I'd filled with water from the kettle. I had braces, acne, and was carrying my customary extra forty pounds. I was dawdling, taking too long, so long that the water in the bucket got cold and the detergent fizzled out to the point of becoming a gray scum on the surface. My brother played our *Best of Bob Marley* CD through the open kitchen window, but even that wasn't improving my mood. My hands were wrinkled and red as I crossed them and leaned heavily on the car roof like a trucker taking a break from his long-haul journey. Our house is tucked within a garden that was, at that time, unruly and overgrown, and that garden is divided by a short avenue on an incline that leads to the front door. I looked down that avenue at the closed iron gates and felt an over-whelming longing for adventure, for something to happen, anything. This longing was underpinned by a deep sense of boredom, that dark sense unique to teenagers that descends without warning and stays for five years.

Idly, I imagined my school crush appearing on his bike at the bottom of the hill and shouting my name. It was unclear if he knew my name at that point—we had never spoken—but this was not based in reality. Even in this fantasy, I wouldn't want to bother him by expecting that he cycle up the hill. I would run to join him, hopping on my bike too, leaving the car's windshield streaked and Bob Marley singing plaintively after me, "Could you be, could you be, could you be loved?" What would happen next was unclear to me, but scarcely mattered. My main thrill came from getting away from this humdrum rural existence crowded with my five sisters and brother, all of whom had the same face as mine, in a house where I always knew what was about to happen next. Of course, today that sounds like paradise, but back then I resented the predictability and safety of it all, and the only way my little brain could imagine an out was via a man, a rescue, a liberating hero. I didn't consider the possibility that I could simply do it myself. That I could hop on my bike and find an adventure, unbidden by a man, or a fourteen-year-old version of a man, whatever they are called. I pictured the scene so vividly, him showing up and taking me away from all of this, that I was surprised when it didn't happen, and quite furious when I found myself jammed in among my sisters in the living room that evening, after the smaller ones had their bath, eating toasted cheese sandwiches and watching *Blind Date*.

Over the course of a romantically disappointing adolescence, my hopes for some kind of deliverance-by-a-hero scenario were firmly put to bed—alone.

Some of the highlights include:

- Slights of the classic "crushes not seeing me at the disco" genre
- Pretty best friend dating crush
- Another pretty, this time male, best friend dating crush
- General unrequited crushes
- Crushing sense of crushes never crushing back

I couldn't figure out how to get a boyfriend until I was twenty-three, and in the meantime I developed a very clever and sturdy streak of self-reliance. I call it the "I'll do it myself," and it's a philosophy stolen from a character in a children's book, the eponymously titled *The Little Red Hen*. The main character, a little red hen, was very independent and found other creatures frustrating to work with. They were too lazy, and didn't help readily, so she huffed about, more than a touch passive-aggressive, and did everything by herself. She constructed bridges, won lawsuits, and made entire five-course dinners by herself, pausing only to trash-talk those around her for not being up to the task. In the end, she alone enjoyed the spoils of her labor. The other animals, those layabouts, would try to crash the party after all the work was done. At that point the Little Red Hen would have her sweet revenge, and hold up one feisty wing and tell them no, this fun part? This, too, she would do herself. You can keep your iconic single women, Carrie Bradshaw, Mindy Lahiri, even Liz Lemon; because my model for living as a successful single woman is a fictitious bird from a children's book.

To go from being single, meaning one, meaning whole, to being *one-half* of a couple, which is, whatever way you look at it, *one-half,* does not sound like a good deal. It sounds like a scam. Or if you're in an open relationship, as an increasing number of my peers are, it sounds like a pyramid scheme. For most of my adult life, I've preferred being single, meaning one, alone, by myself. My modus operandi is mano a mano with Maeve-o. While ineptitude and laziness turn the little red hen and me right off, in her case she seems to doubt that *anyone* can do anything right. In my case, it isn't that I suspect the capability of men to make a good partner. There are a million perfectly wonderful men out there. Out of nine billion. Honestly, I mean, look at DJ Khaled—one glance at his social media would restore the most cynical of women's faith in men. All day long, in between enjoying his garden and doing good work in the community, he sings to and cuddles his wife and their baby. Men can sometimes do a great job!

Other times, they can't. Many women have reservations the size of reservations about their husbands or boyfriends, but they put them aside and hold on tight to their man, as if we are still back in Jane Austen's day. I know some of these women; you will find a list of their names on my website, www.foundmymrcollins.co. conflicted. From my high and single horse, I feel that they would be better off alone, I think they should do it themselves. I get it, though; mortgages are expensive, Sundays are long, social pressure is high. And it's nice to get that life department all cleared up and ready to hibernate in for the winter, even if it is in the basement and there's no central heating and one time a crow got in and you're not sure if it ever flew back out again.

Being alone is great for all the small stuff: seeing whatever you want at the movies, eating in that weird way you can only eat by yourself, going on vacation wherever you like. Being alone is ideal for eavesdropping, for really relaxing, and, at times, for forcing me to be sociable. And, in truth, being alone is great for the big stuff too. I have yet to go through an illness or a loss or a nuclear war, knock on wood, without a partner, and perhaps I would change my tune if I had to. Actually, what am I talking about? At the first hint of real trouble I would immediately step up my campaign to meet and marry Michael Fassbender. Be that as it may, I do know that being alone has been good for my version of big stuff: moving countries, being a writer, and hanging huge portraits of Beyoncé and Serena in my living room.

I know that many people dread the prospect of being alone; they fear that the solitude will magnify their flaws and force them to face up to who they really are.

But the funny thing I've discovered is that being alone can actually be a way of escaping who you are, or who you think you are, a chance to make up new versions, better versions. I'm not talking about the witness protection program here, rather the gentle way you can surprise yourself, the way that is too easily undone by a companion with a set idea of how you should be. I've found that being alone allows me to become part of a place, to somehow melt into the fabric of it, however foreign I may be to that place. When I am alone, nobody will say, however fondly, *It's so like you to say that, Maeve.* Or, *Hmm, I didn't think you'd like Turkish coffee.* I've been to all sorts of places—a dumpling house in Melbourne, a wedding in Brooklyn, a public park in Shiraz—and I have really been there, really experienced them. Those places have absorbed me without question, because I was able to disperse myself among them. I was not this whole formed thing, this solid block, I was just floating particles that formed and reformed as they wished or needed to, with no clear set of rules, nobody else's expectations to act into.

I've always been this way, wincing when a barista recognizes me and shouts my order down the line. My nightmare gift is a box of tiny thoughtful gifts collected by an earnest boyfriend. You know, a book I read and loved at fourteen, a handful of all-yellow Jelly Babies, a framed photo of my nieces, and, God forbid, some kind of mixtape! I would say thank you, politely, eyes shining with fear that he would mistake for gratitude, then I'd excuse myself and jump right out of the closest window. I don't want to be scrutinized like a set of blueprints, I want to be off by myself, alone in my thoughts, able to vanish whenever I need to.

I grew up sharing a room with three of my sisters, in a house on a small island where both of my parents' families lived too, all of us just off another small island, Ireland. With aunts and uncles, cousins and family friends, I had a typically idyllic Irish childhood and I was never alone. I still wonder at the relief I feel when I am alone, because I didn't hate that life at all. Today, it's a pure pleasure to visit Cobh and have old ladies stop me outside the shop we used to get ice-cream cones from as children, and tell me I look like my grandmother, and ask which one of the Higgins girls I am. It's incredibly comforting to have a doctor who vaccinated me as a baby, who knows my entire extended family's medical history, who prescribed me birth control as a teenager (for acne, naturally), ask me how I'm doing, how I'm really doing. So why, then, do I crave a silent apartment, a train crowded with strangers, a forty-block walk where hundreds of people will see me but nobody will really look? I'm not sure what it is I need this anonymity for; it's not as if I got to New York and felt, *Aha, now I'm finally free to kill!* But living in this city, so far from where

I was born, feels like a rare and precious freedom, one I sense is not afforded to many women in the world. But freedom from what? I can't seem to say, it's just that my personality's instant response to anything and everything is a little-red-hen-style shimmy and a quick, *I'll do it myself.*

That being said, something odd has been happening. On occasion, throughout this past year, I've begun to cross over from the highness of aloneness to the lowness of loneliness. It's a deeply unpleasant feeling, that one of not being enough on my own, of neediness. It lasts somewhere between ten minutes and a day at a time. This loneliness occurs at predictable moments, like an ill-planned holiday weekend when I remember too late that the library is closed, and I have cramps, and I find myself thinking about people who are thousands of miles away, and I badly need a hug. It creeps up on me at unexpected moments and takes what I think are unfair opportunities, like when I've done something really great and I want to talk about how great that thing was, and how well I did it, and how nobody in the world could've handled it like I just did. I want to relive it and embellish it and have some outside voice comment on just how glorious I am! You know, everyday modest appraisal of my actions. But my friends are caught up in their own particular lives and don't always have time to amplify mine.

More and more, dotted throughout the shabby couples on view, I notice a few who really work well together, people who add to each other's lives instead of subtracting. I asked my little sister, the one who used to be a sunny baby who is now a sunny adult about to move in with her boyfriend, just what it is that she appreciates about being in a couple. She said that when she was sick the previous week, her boyfriend rubbed her back and made sugary tea, and she felt embarrassed at first but he was so kind that she stopped feeling that way. Only true love can battle away an Irishwoman's innate embarrassment. She also told me that it's helpful to have someone in your life who can gently suggest you may be overthinking a situation that isn't as complicated as you think. I assured her that I do not have a problem with overthinking. "I'm not prone to that, I'm a person of action, unafraid of anything!" I insisted before we finished Skyping. I then went immediately to the nearest body of water, the lake in Prospect Park, and sat cross-legged on the ground, staring at the water until both of my legs went dead, thinking.

I thought about a cure for loneliness and about trying something different because what I'm doing now isn't working anymore, and I thought about not being afraid and also about how I tend to overthink things, so perhaps it was time for action. *This is settled*, I told myself, *I'll do it myself, must find "The One." Or at least one of the ones.* I tell my married friend Shaina that I'm about to commence my search. And while she is very happy with her choices and life, she warns me to enjoy my time being single because, "Once you meet someone and it's right, then, bam! You're sleeping in your living room and you have a kid." She's quiet on the phone for a while before adding, "And you have to constantly think about how many pastries your spouse is consuming, for his own sake." Hoping that is specific to her, I am undeterred, and I make a plan.

What type of person am I looking for? Someone like my father, as Freud would have wanted? Every little sixty-year-old in construction gear with a gray mustache catches my eye. A van full of roofers passes by and the elderly driver looks rattled by my intense stare. I don't think that's how I'll find my guy, but it does give me an idea, another children's book, this time the opposite of the little red hen and her fierce thirst for independence. It's called *Are You My Mother?* and it features the harrowing story of another bird, a baby bird this time, who wakes up alone and spends most of the book going from creature to creature asking, "Are you my mother?" I know who my mother is, she is a hyperactive grandmother who, right now, is probably rifling through an odds-and-ends bin in a charity shop, looking for busted-up teddies to repair. My husband, though, who is that? Is it efficient to take the direct approach, marching up to every man to ask "Are you my husband?" Surely not, for there are absolutely millions of them.

I must focus, and narrow it down, so I sit up in bed with my notebook on a Sunday morning and write down what it is I'm looking for. The person:

- Must be funny and good at impressions.
- Maybe can cook?
- Can make pancakes but with coconut flour but not too eggy.
- Can make coffee or doesn't mind going to get coffee from that nice place on Seventh Avenue.
- Maybe would go and get a nice coffee from that place and get the paper too, then come back and make coconut pancakes and have some raspberries with them.

I soon realize I'm more focused on planning my morning, specifically my breakfast, than on finding true love. That "funny" thing, though, there's a clue to go on. I highly doubt my husband is a comedian, because the sad truth of the matter is that we comedians are brittle oddballs, and I need exclusive rights to that behavior in whatever couple I end up in. I want him to be funny but also stable, maybe like a successful ophthalmologist who crosses his own eyes when he tells you to follow his pen.

Stepping onto the dating field makes me feel like a

discus thrower, and the discus is my self-esteem. Everything bad I believe about myself, true and false, comes
rushing to the surface and I get scared. My friend Claudia says it's all in my head. She urges me to *act as if*, to
act as if I'm a hot piece of ass. That way I'll convince
others, and then they'll come a-tappin'. Claudia is tiny
and pretty, and it's annoying to hear from her on the
subject. She persists, though, sending me a video of an
unfortunate woman who had her face bitten off by an
ape and has to live in a nursing home as a result, yet who
still managed to find love. In the end she won her piano
teacher over with her indomitable personality and adorable efforts to master the piano. They are engaged to be
married and I notice that I'm glad for this lady with no
face and a proficiency on the keys, but I'm not about to
reverse-engineer her relationship trajectory to find one
of my own. I do find myself dawdling near the tamarin
cages at Prospect Park Zoo, but that's not out of some
misguided wish to have my face bitten off, it's because
the keeper looks cute. I picture our life together: me
keeping the vegetable peelings in a little butter tub so he
can take them to work and make friends with the mon-
keys; him teaching me about nature in simple, allegori-
cal ways that help me to finally understand the world.
When I shake myself out of my reverie he is nowhere to
be seen.

   Time passes, and I do what the baby bird does. I look

up. I look down. I fall very far down, out of my nest on the top of the tree, and down onto the ground. I search and search. The worst part is that the baby bird actually strolled right by his mother early on in his journey. He was so busy looking for her, he didn't see her. I worry that I've missed my husband already, or I could miss him today—I could walk right by him and not see him! Other fears crowd in. What if he's married to someone else? Could I calmly explain the mix-up? Get some apology tulips for his first wife? Maybe he's in prison, forever. Should I visit prisons? Maybe he lives in Mongolia. I was supposed to go there a few years ago, to visit my brother, but I was sick and had to cancel my trip. Somewhere beyond Ulaanbaatar sits a lonely goatherd, looking out of a yurt to the steppe beyond; is he waiting for me?

The baby bird trips along, running into a kitten and then a cow and asking, "Are you my mother?" each time. I come across equally ludicrous creatures, and try to lower the pitch of my skepticism to give them a shot. "Are you my husband?" I ask an unhappy writer in Des Moines. He just looks and looks and does not say a thing. I ask a mean young surgeon on the Upper East Side, "Are you my husband?" *Absolutely not,* he responds, in a number of ways. "What about you?" I ask a vaguely interesting handyman. He looks at me the same way the cow looked at the baby bird, like, *No, ma'am, absolutely not*. I panic. Do I even have a husband? I do, I know I do! I have to find him! The baby bird panics too, and calls out to boats and airplanes, almost pleading. He is increasingly desperate, to the point of putting himself in a dangerous situation with some kind of forklift truck. I'm not in physical danger, but I'm quite far out, and teetering. That's fine. Because in the end, the baby bird finds his mother. He manages to make his way back to the top of the tree, and she simply appears, and when she does, he doesn't even need to ask who she is, he just knows.

How Funny

MY NIECE IS NOT YET TWO. We are in my parents' garden, one-third of an acre around their old farmhouse in Cobh. The landscape is always changing, because of the seasons, of course, but mainly because of my father's constant tipping. Tipping is what he calls working, and that can mean anything from deadheading a bed of daffodils to showing up in a borrowed excavator and digging a giant hole for a septic tank. Either way, he wears a blue onesie with reinforced knees and goes about his business. The one thing he is not allowed to do is set fire to anything, following an incident with gasoline and branches shorn from an unfortunate horse chestnut tree that left his eyelashes singed but eyebrows perfectly arched.

For most of my childhood there was a huge thicket of

gooseberry bushes on one side of the avenue leading up to the house, and beside it stood a rickety swing set whose entire frame lurched as you swung, enhancing the thrill by making it actually dangerous. A huge eucalyptus tree dominated the other side. That silvery-barked giant is gone now, and the gooseberry bushes have been replaced with a grow tunnel for vegetables and a luxury wooden swing set for the grandchildren to ignore while they play in the grow tunnel. So, the baby is in the grow tunnel in *her* blue onesie with reinforced knees and she bends down, diapered butt in the air, pudgy tanned hands pressing into the soil, and takes a deep sniff of a head of lettuce. It has no smell, really, she's pretending it's a flower. I recognize this at once, she's doing a bit. "Gorgeous," she lisps, and waits for the laugh, which comes rolling in like thunder, thunder made out of giggles.

In my family, being funny is prized, like sporting medals are in other families. You may note how unfamiliar I am with sports because I use the term "sporting medals" like a robot pretending to be a football player. At least a poor robot wouldn't get some weird brain injury that allows him to keep his job while beating his girlfriend. But that's a whole other story, one for the NFL to tell in its own book of hilarious essays. Being funny was and is my family's touchdown, our goal, our certificate of achievement. This explains the baby making the lettuce gag, and our reaction to it as adults. My sister, the child's mother, laughs and builds on it, as she must; I mean, it's a pretty weak gag. "Oh, what a beautiful flower! Will I pick this and put it in a vase?" The baby, cracking up over this, points at another lettuce and says, "Fow-fow?" She means flower. I nod vigorously. "Oooh, another flower—so many flowers in here, we must tell Grandad." We pick the lettuce and later, in the kitchen, my father gets involved, thanking her profusely for the flowers, fussing about finding a vase. She watches this pantomime, rapt.

Has she really created some alternate reality that we are all trapped in now, where lettuce is a flower and grown-ups believe anything you tell them? Then there's the "wait a second" moment when he suddenly notices these aren't flowers at all! She stands there—thrilled, a little bit scared, did she push the joke too far? Will Grandad be angry? He shakes his head, marveling at how he was deceived, then he bursts out laughing, and tells her she is very clever and very funny. She is giddy and relieved and feeling great about the whole routine, so she tries it again. I stand in the doorway, arms folded, it's all so familiar. I'm an old-timer on the scene, vaping up these fumes languidly, watching my baby girl achieve that delicious first high. The family babies know that the golden goose is a laugh, and they're always chasing it, happy to fall over if that will help them get it faster.

Comedy is our gift and our curse. Another niece is

five, and is so bright and quick and funny that I sometimes worry for her. I know how her brain fizzles and
snaps two things together to make a joke, whether or
not she wants it to. She can't help zipping in with a line,
and having a smart mouth is not always a smart move.
More than once I've noticed an aggression that comes
over some men when I'm funny, even when I'm not being funny at their expense. I shivered with recognition
when I first read something Margaret Atwood said
while speaking at a university in 1982. "Why do men
feel threatened by women?" I asked a male friend of
mine. "They're afraid women will laugh at them," he
said. "Undercut their worldview." Then I asked some
women students in a quickie poetry seminar I was giving, "Why do women feel threatened by men?" "They're
afraid of being killed," they said. I believe it all. As I
write this, the Justice Department is gearing up to retry
a woman named Desiree Fairooz, who was accused of
laughing at Attorney General Jeff Sessions during his
confirmation hearing. She was convicted of disorderly
conduct and sentenced to a year in prison, but that sentence was dismissed by a judge, so Sessions is going after her again.

Putting aside my anxieties for my funny little niece
and the potential danger therein, it's wonderful to see her
discover her superpower. Once, as we all sat down for
lunch, around fifteen people, my five-year-old nephew,

her cousin, who was learning about King Arthur, said, "Grandad is at the top of the table, like the king" and she responded, "And you're the queen," garnering an almost involuntary laugh from all of us. The two babies sitting on laps didn't get the joke, but they laughed along. They always laugh along, pretending that they do get it. The queen quip hurt her cousin a bit; he's not keen on being called anything remotely girl-like. "No, I'm not the queen," he said, unable to think of a better comeback. His little brother laughed a lot, looking adoringly at the joker. It is that edge, the slightly serrated edge of many jokes, that make them so irresistible, maybe so natural. If there's a pecking order, pecking is in order if you want to get to the top of it. "That's a bit mean, love," said her mother dutifully. My niece's tiny eyebrows furrowed for a second, she glanced guiltily at her cousin, but she had that post-joke glow that she definitely wasn't about to lose in a hurry.

I watch these babies grow up, straining to understand punch lines, eager to decipher the codes that make adults go from serious to silly. They learn that if something is not funny, you can make it funny. They remind me of myself, not just because they look exactly like me, with dark curls, sturdy limbs, and friendly faces, but because they are as demented as an alchemist, trying every day to turn whatever dull material is served up to them into glittering comedy gems.

My comedy apple didn't fall far from the tree either. My mother called me recently, an unusual event in itself due to her unfortunate relationship with technology. I was on a deadline, but closed my laptop and answered the call, wondering if I should be worried. She talked about the weather, mentioned an upcoming christening, and asked me how my back was. I'd hurt my back months earlier and it was completely better. She seemed on edge and I couldn't figure out the real reason for her call. I ticked off possibilities in my head as we chitchatted. Had I missed a birthday, an anniversary? Had I written something that could have annoyed her? Finally, I said I had a lot of work to do, and her voice got higher as she came out with the real reason for her call. She practically squealed. "Did you get the picture of the octopus?" I hadn't, and didn't know what she meant. After much confusion that included some remote iPhone guidance from me, five thousand miles away, it emerged that my mother believed she'd sent me a photo of an octopus. She did this to freak me out, because she knows how those eight-legged underwater ghouls terrify me. She had long promised to send me a statue of a china dog, one with a great backstory. I was waiting for that, so when she had sent a message with the octopus photo (neither of which I had received) saying *Here's your new friend for the shelf!*, she told me she thought I'd think it was a photo of the china dog and that would lure me into opening the photo. I didn't have the heart to tell her that you don't have to "open" photos that someone texts to you, because she was already feeling stupid, and worrying about who she actually sent the photo to. "I hope it wasn't one of the people from the Quaker meeting, but I suppose I'll never find out now." My mother, crazed from waiting for a reaction to her prank, had called me because she couldn't stand the thought of her hilarious gag going unseen.

Funny people are my favorite, maybe because they feel like home. Let me be clear: by funny people I absolutely do not mean comedians. Some comedians are funny, of course. Some of my favorite people are comedians! But, sadly, most comedians are not really funny as much as confident/persistent/sociopathic in their mimicry of actual funniness. The most deeply unfunny people I know are comedians, and earn a good living from it too. I don't begrudge them their success, but I do dislike them. I have one of those unfortunate faces that betrays what the brain behind it is thinking, so I've learned never to sit near a light at a comedy club, lest my wincing and frowning put one or more of my colleagues off their well-worn, tedious stride. The people I hold dearest are the ones who are funny for funny's sake. They do bits without a microphone, they deliver punch lines silently to themselves, they joke around without any obvious reward. They are the bus driver who consistently responds to the question, "How much is the bus?" with a deadpan, "About two hundred and fifty thousand dollars." They are the science teacher Photoshopping baby goats onto his wife's birthday card, and the seven-year-old pulling a goofy face in the mirror that only she will see.

Now, a great many flattering crowns are bestowed upon the Irish. Best storytellers, best accents, even best terrorists (they *always* phoned ahead). Visitors to the Emerald Isle, so-called because the people are so pale they are almost green, sing ecstatically in praise of the literature, the banter, and the butter. All of those things are truly worthy of that praise, and difficult to choose between. If you put a gun to my head, or to my knees, as the great gentlemen of the IRA were prone to do, I suppose I would choose banter. I truly do find a great proportion of Irish people extremely funny. I'm not interested in Irish jokes; in any case I rarely hear them, on account of me being Irish. It's certainly a blow to my ego when non-Irish people tell me that everything I say in my accent is funny, but I concede there is something about Irishness that lends itself to being funny. It's surely too simple to say that in Ireland we are emotionally constipated and humor is a laxative. But don't jokes help our compacted feelings come flooding out of our bodies, in this case our mouths, often in a big rush of relief? I believe they do. Irish people have a particular sense of humor, one that is easy and fun for me to slip back into when I'm there. Slagging off and messing with and cutting down, I love it! Despite its obvious post-colonization, chip-on-the-shoulder, little-guy meanness, I love it and I'm good at it. We partake in it a lot in my family. It's comfortable but slightly scary, like a warm pool perfect for splashing around in, without ever fully relaxing, because you know there are unseen creatures at the bottom ready to nip your toes.

For better or worse, across continents and time zones, the bonds created by affectionate teasing, fortified by the long-term tormenting of one another, only seem to strengthen. I currently have a brother and a sister in the Middle East and a sister in London; everyone else lives in Ireland, specifically in Cobh, where we all grew up. One July day I was on Twitter when a *New York Times* journalist tweeted that she was in Central Park and there had been an explosion, with at least one person injured. Chatter quickly swirled up through social media of the explosion being some kind of terrorist attack, maybe just the first incident of many that would unfold that day. I thought immediately of my family, that as soon as they heard they would quickly develop that "I'm sure it's fine . . . but" feeling, the one that comes over us all when we hear about a terrorist attack occurring near a loved one. We have a family WhatsApp group, usually used to share photos of our nieces and nephews. Oh, and one octopus, since my mother learned that WhatsApp is a little more reliable than texts when something is urgent. I sent a message to everyone immediately.

> You might see on the news there's been a terrorist attack in Central Park, but I'm fine, nowhere near there, loads of love xxx

Minutes later, the same journalist reported that what had happened was not a terrorist attack, but an accident. An unfortunate man had somehow stepped on a firework in Central Park and injured his leg. After the news had righted itself, it was quickly forgotten on social media. Not so on my family WhatsApp group. One sister wrote six minutes after my initial panicky message, and the replies came flooding in after her.

> **Sister 1:** Oh I doubt we'll see it on the news Maeve 😂😂😂 it was just a fireworks accident
> **Sister 2:** Are your likkle ears ok after the big naughty bang Sisty?
> **Sister 3:** 😂 😂 😂
> **Sister 1 again:** #nowherenearthere
> **Sister 2:** smh the drama!!! #pray4newyork
> **Sister 3:** 😂 😂 😂

And so on and so forth, for many days to follow. I tried everything to make them stop teasing me: threats, guilt, numerous links to various terrible things that happened in New York that week, like murders and robberies and this one rat getting on a subway car and jumping on a sleeping man's face. None of it helped. They continued to mock me for being a scaredy-cat, an alarmist, for the sheer ego I'd displayed in imagining I may somehow be caught up in a terrorist attack.

In our hometown, the Cobh Regatta, a series of sailing competitions, happens each August. There's also a Bonnie Baby Competition, a Kayak Duck Hunt (kayakers compete to catch as many ducks as possible), and a local taxi driver/opera singer performing on the bandstand. Because of the Central Park false alarm, I had reason to dread that year's regatta. Not for any of the aforementioned activities, but rather because the regatta's finale is always a gorgeous fireworks display in the harbor. I knew what was coming. I would be in New York, but I counted down the minutes nonetheless. And sure enough, right on time, ten p.m. Irish time, five p.m. New York time, as I sat in a Pret A Manger eating a miserable quinoa salad, the WhatsApp group lit up. Numerous family members sent photos of themselves making scared faces, backlit by fireworks, alongside assurances that although I might see this on the news, they were all fine and sending me #loadsoflove.

Many months later, there were early reports of a terrorist attack in London. Naturally, for the people involved, I hoped it wasn't true. I also hoped that it wasn't true so that my sister who lived there would check in too early and be mocked like I was. Sadly, it was true. As soon as the police commissioner spoke about the attacks on BBC news, my sister deemed it safe enough to check in. Immediately after he confirmed it was the fault of the terrorists, she messaged to reassure the WhatsApp group that she was fine, at home in her apartment and #nowherenearthere. And, like the last line of every cheesy sitcom script, we all laughed, even the dog.

A joke can be many things: a simple play on words to delight another person, a break from the mundanity of a day, or a code to let someone know that you know what they're up to, that you approve, that you disapprove. Being funny is a way of being indirect too, skirting around the ugly feelings, not saying what you mean because what you mean is too big, too painful. In our case, the rounds of messages were really saying, *Nothing bad will ever happen to you, it simply cannot, because we all love you so much.*

I count myself lucky to come from a funny family like mine, from a funny place like Ireland. I like myself best when I'm being funny. Naturally I am drawn to melancholy, and anxiety is always rapping on my brain-door. Stories of human frailty and cruelty obsess me, so actually deliberately being funny feels wonderfully powerful. Some days being funny just happens, but most days it's a decision and, if I can muster it, an action. Those days, when it really works, feel incredible. I feel like the boss and creator and queen of this whole Earth. I have a memory of walking toward a podium to do a reading in a theater, and in the memory my skin is shining golden and the light coming from within me makes people stare. I feel so solid on my feet, so secure in the knowledge that all the universal forces will obey me, I could float right up and not be in any danger. I may even need to float up to that open sky because I will fill it all, glowing and expanding the way I am. I'm thrilled that people are paying attention, because I'm about to be funny. I want to hear them too, because I can understand them now. We all commune and it's right and wise and beautiful that I'm able to share this light at last.

And then there are other days, more days, when I feel like a prehistoric creature, a sort of giant sunken toad, very still and quiet, concealed underneath layers of silt and murky water. I'm okay, not sad or worried. I'm just there, breathing in and out through my gills. People poke at me with different sticks. Duty sticks, fun sticks, work sticks. Those sticks elicit a reaction that gets harder to reproduce each time. Heavy-lidded, I smile blearily up at the people wielding them. "Oh, hey," I say, trying to get the thickness out of my voice, like when you answer the phone too soon after sleep.

"Sorry, I meant to call you." Days spent above on the shore become long days of trying to fake it till I make it, make it back down below. How tiring it is, acting like a person on dry land! Words I say that I do not mean, faces I arrange to convince a friend, promises I make just to put something off.

I cling to jokes when I feel that toad lurking, hoping their buoyancy will keep me above ground, or at least disguise the fact that I'm sinking. Because the toad is so horribly ugly, I'm determined that nobody close to me will find out that it's there, waiting patiently under the little islands I'm hopping to and from, bound to absorb me. Funniness is the perfect evasion tactic, keeping me afloat for a little while longer, and convincing others I'm safe. That said, time has proven that the people who know me best soon add extreme funniness to the other signs that I am about to enter toad mode, the one-plus-two of unwashed hair and unanswered emails. That's when the concern sticks appear, prodding and jostling me to react. Sometimes the sticks are useful, I can catch hold of one and haul myself back up to the shore, but sometimes they push me farther down.

When I can no longer summon the funny, I go quiet. Eventually, all the sticks stop working and, with a minimum of fuss, the toad swallows me whole and we drop back through the swamp and down into the muddy water again, where it's muffled and cool. On days like that, an adrenaline shot straight to my heart could have only one response. A polite, exhausted, "Oh, thank you, yes, I do feel better." I stay there, the sticks cannot reach down this far, the voices above are faint and unimportant. My toad brain explains that it's best for everyone this way, I don't want to get my slime on their nice dresses, do I? And nobody will ever find out that I'm anything other than a ray of sunshine, a laugh a minute, an easy companion, and a really fun time.

I read once, in *National Geographic*, about a city called Vrindavan in India, around a hundred miles south of Delhi, a place known as a "city of widows." Thousands of widows have moved there, either by choice or because their community has shunned them for being tainted and burdensome. A psychologist named Vasantha Patri was quoted as saying that many widows are "physically alive but socially dead." When I read that, a light went on, or rather off, because to me, that is exactly what depression feels like. "Feels like" are the operative words, of course; my situation is a thousand times easier than an unfortunate poverty-stricken widow who has been abandoned by society. And when I'm settled in the silt, if it's not exactly a self-imposed exile, it's a toad-imposed one. Nobody outside of the marsh has forced me to shut up about my depression, at least not for a long time. Now it's just me and the toad, and we don't want to be a drag.

You know how, when you're trying to clean up your act and eat right, the soundest advice is to shop around the perimeter of the grocery store? That that's where you'll find the freshest greens and loveliest fruits, where you'll find everything you need to make a delicious smoothie that everybody enjoys? Well, that's how I treat emotions: the healthy ones are around the edges, they are easy to identify and so good for you! I vow to never venture into the middle aisles where the bad stuff is. That's the poison, the indulgent stuff, the bad emotions that can only be used on special occasions, as a treat! But, of course, it's not up to me to decide what to feel, or is it?

After a long time in the silence, I forget who is who, me or the toad. Perhaps we're the same, I note without feeling, as the heaviness grows and I note, again without feeling, that I need help carrying it. Not for the first time, I ask for that help from the same doctor who gave me my vaccinations as a baby, and saw me pass through all the stages my little funny nieces are passing through today. I sit in his office and explain that I'm subterranean once more. He nods his head, gray by now, encourages me to look after myself, and agrees to renew my prescription for antidepressants. I ask him if he remembers vaccinating me, and if he thinks those vaccinations caused this mental illness. I say that to him as a topical joke, because the anti-vaccination movement is picking up steam and I want him to think I'm funny and I want one of us to get a laugh out of this. The doctor duly delivers a laugh, despite, or maybe because of, the croaking recitation of my swampy woes that preceded the joke.

Small Talk

IN THE FOUR YEARS I've lived in the U.S., I have grown used to excruciatingly sincere exchanges with people. Within minutes of meeting you, they'll come up with the heavy goods, and expect to see yours in return. *I guess what I'm afraid of is that my husband is bored with me. Also, in case you're wondering what that sound is? I have digestion issues.* Americans are good at a great many things: drone warfare, making cherry-flavored jellies taste more like cherries than cherries themselves, optimism. But they struggle with small talk. In Ireland, small talk is just that—I mean, it's tiny.

At the beginning of a three-hour train trip from Dublin to Cork, I will spend an average of fifteen minutes comfortably discussing the merits of having a café car on the train with the middle-aged man beside me. *I suppose, if you're peckish, it's ideal, really.* A nice pause. *Or if you didn't have time to bring some food with you from home, it's absolutely perfect. But the tea costs more than my ticket.* Eyes widen and head nods in agreement. *But you can't dip chocolate in your ticket.* A chuckle. Nothing meaningful, at least on the surface. After that, we do our work, read our books, look out the window. What the seemingly meaningless exchange means is we can relax. The person we're inches away from for the afternoon is not dangerous. We can easily say, "'Scuse me," and not be glared at when we need to get something from the overhead shelf, or go to the famed café car. At the end of the trip we'll nod and smile, and I won't be left wondering why his father said that one thing in 1994 that meant he never had the confidence to pursue a career in architecture.

Every culture has its own version of small talk, another full language that you must learn if you wish to fit in. For one long and miserable year I lived in London, and experimented with the English version of small talk. It's similar to Ireland's in its skillful adherence to the proper dimensions of chitchat, that is, they keep it small, but it doesn't have the same sweet aftertaste, the same warmth. I'm not interested in furthering the whole "the Irish are cuddly servants and the English are frigid colonizers" nonsense, all I'm saying is the small talk is different. The English are, famously, wonderfully reserved and exquisitely polite. I find that remarkable, considering their forefathers used to maraud around the world touching people and objects and countries, shouting, "Tip, I tipped it, I got it! It's mine now. I own it!" But as I say, the history is unimportant. I'm sticking to the subject of small talk, remember? The following is an example of the carefully managed conversation style they have, in the form of this classic exchange with a production assistant as we waited for a meeting to start.

Me: This rain! Will it ever end?
Englishwoman: Well, it must, mustn't it?
Me: Hope so, my hair is so frizzy! Anyway, I hate my hair.
Englishwoman: (*faraway tone*) To think that we wash our hair in water, but we duck out of the rain to keep it dry.

She did not respond well to my self-deprecating remark about my hair. An Irish person, even a bald one, would have told me that they hate their hair too. It's kind of gross, I know, but bonding over low-key self-loathing is an important part of our Constitution and an Irish person can be sued by the state and/or the Church for being "too confident-seeming." I'm joking, but it was illegal to like yourself before 1979 in one of those "don't ask, don't tell" sort of ways. In any case, the Irish actually do share a lot with the British—a penchant for binge drinking, a drizzly climate, and, of course, that famous border.

I appreciate that we both prefer not to go hard on the personal stuff up top and am convinced that the English are even more closed off than the Irish. I mean, even the throwaway hair comment I made was a little much for my new English friend. These days I think fondly of the careful verbal dances done back in that mildewed little country, particularly when confronted with the straight-talking, all-out-in-the-openness of my new countrymen. If I utter something about hating my hair here, or anything even vaguely down on myself, a kindly American with a concerned face is sure to pipe up with a dozen concerned questions and assurances and perhaps even a "Thank you so much for sharing that with me."

Small talk can and must happen everywhere in a city where you don't know a lot of people. While I reject the label "party animal," I absolutely accept "party balloon animal," aka "Yung S'mores," aka me. I love kids' parties, and during my first year here as a babysitter I went to lots of them, despite my fear of clowns. I'm not afraid of clowns because of their electric hand buzzers or flowers that spray water or even those pervasive "clowns are murderers" rumors. I'm afraid of clowns because they went to college, and traveled, and sometimes they even worked as actors in France, then they moved to New York to make a life for themselves as a creative person, and now they sell weed or walk dogs to pay rent. I guess I'm afraid of failure. I didn't go to college, and I was only in France for the pastries, and I moved to New York to make a life for myself as a creative person, so what will happen to me? Anyway, I keep those thoughts to myself at kids' parties, and focus on the things I love, like the ice-cream cakes shaped like animals, the dearth of boring work talk, and, of course, that special low-level hysteria caused by sugar that I absolutely excel at.

The last kids' birthday party I attended was one of those where the adults stick around and it kind of blends into the evening. I was chatting with this one cool-guy dad with a pale ale in his hand, and he opened up within thirty seconds. *Something people don't talk about enough is how hard parenting really is, and sometimes you're just not going to like your kids.* All I'd asked was whether he'd been on the bouncy castle yet. I didn't have the heart to tell him that, actually, two other people at the same party had said more or less the same thing to me just minutes earlier. Was this disgruntled trio just unlucky, with a slew of particularly unlikable children between them? No! They were simply saying what was on their minds. You see, nothing is too personal, there's nothing people don't talk about. That should come as a relief to me, growing up in a repressed, Catholic country where my mother explained rape to us as *when someone loves you, but you don't want them to*. In truth, this extraordinary level of openness I find in America is a relief, but it also feels like a little loss.

I understand that openness beats secrecy, taboos should be challenged, and indirectness is baffling. It's just that I don't always want to dive right in. When someone opens big, and I don't feel ready to get among their guts, of course I'm polite about it. I nod along, I try to appreciate their candor, at the same time hoping something will happen to distract them, like maybe their hair will catch fire from a candle or a pug will appear and know some tricks. Those incidents are both wonderful conversation starters. "Oh, what hair spray do you use? It seems flammable," or "I never knew dogs could read braille." Sadly, they are also highly unlikely. Long-haired people are ever more aware of the danger of open flames, and pugs are largely both sighted *and* lazy. I miss the small talk.

At times, in a new place, I've felt like a little billy goat trying to make friends, butting my head against oblivious knees, bleating out all the hits, knowing there is nothing more off-putting than this neediness I'm feeling. When I moved to New York, I was determined not to do this. Instead of being a billy goat, I was a lioness. Potential friends were the billy goats. I would survey them in groups, single out the ones I liked, then pursue them until they got tired enough to slow down and chat. To make real friends you need to get to know somebody, and let them get to know you, so I tried to remember how to do that. I grew up on an island off an island, so many of my friendships have a solid base of familiarity that I don't remember forming. Many of the people dearest to me have known me since Junior Infants. (In Ireland, first grade is called Junior Infants, and second grade is called Senior Infants, or in some case Low Babies and High Babies. *I know!*)

I soon figured out that to make real friends I needed to have real conversations with people, to spend actual time with them. It's like dating: small talk needs to get big at some stage, so perhaps I should not complain about these deep and meaningful questions being tossed around at first sight. The brutal truth is that time and energy are resources, and New Yorkers never have enough of either because of capitalism and self-absorption, so their technique, inasmuch as they have one, is to get straight to it. I'm fanatically curious about other people and I, too, want to know all sorts of things about strangers, but there's something off-putting about how quickly and carelessly the prodding begins.

Besides, believing and acting on this no-nonsense "who exactly are you?" school of conversation neglects the fact that small talk, when done correctly, is an extremely efficient way of getting to know somebody. You may not find out where they work, or who they know, or whether they have a good relationship with their family, but you'll get some idea of *them*, the person, that odd-shaped part of a human being that's invisible to the eye and impossible to articulate. You know, their spleen or spirit or personality or whatever doctors call it nowadays. Are they kind, hurting, silly, bad? Some combination of all of those? You can find out, if you ask them about the party food, or tell them about your subway ride, or bring up the oddly cloudless sky outside, and simply take it from there.

I found one of my good friends when, right after we were introduced, he said in a low voice, "I'm just over here trying to get my chip-to-dip ratio right; not sure you can help me with that." I was all in. We talked about layered dip for a solid fifteen minutes, and while it won't play well on paper, I assure you it was both fun and informative. It somehow led to him telling me that Vladimir Putin has fillers in his cheeks, and to us discussing the cosmetic surgery we wanted. Not in a serious way, not at all. He wants an extra elbow put in so he can wave around doors after he's left the room, and I want eyes surgically placed at the back of my head, peeping out from just over my ponytail. I appreciate that factual information is crucial in order for us to understand the world around us, but there's plenty of time and opportunities for that. The real mystery, the one we should be most curious about, is just what exactly is going on in someone else's mind and heart. The best parts of a person are buried too deep to be uncovered by as blunt an instrument as a direct question.

My first year here was a busy round of collecting and processing: new people, new places, new foods. I mean, it took me almost a week to recover from the existence of this one particular chicken torta at my local Mexican place. That's not some kind of scatological joke, it's an astonishingly good sandwich that I planned my day around for a week. I was full of gratitude for my new city, and determined to make the most of every opportunity it offered. To live in this fast, beautiful, ambitious city, I would have to take on those qualities.

As is the way of an all-or-nothing brain, I developed a dual obsession. I wrote on my refrigerator, in permanent Sharpie, that I needed to *GIVE BACK AND GET IN SHAPE*. In one fateful twenty-minute Google session, I applied for a yoga teacher training course and a mentoring program for girls. I was accepted into both. The latter proved to be one of the greatest decisions ever made in the history of womankind. Instead of being upset about not being supported in my work, I started supporting others. It worked really well, still does, even if it does sometimes involve my editing thirty thousand words of sci-fi fan fiction about characters I will never understand.

The yoga teacher training course, however, was a disaster. Now, before you slam this book shut in disgust at my complaining about a yoga teacher training course I paid $3,000 to take, please know that it abruptly ended six weeks later, at least for me, right after I slipped two disks in a very deep forward fold I should definitely not have tried. But that was all ahead of me. The same week in September saw the first day of both courses, yoga on Saturday mornings, mentoring on Saturday afternoons. It was all falling into place; soon I'd be some kind of supple superhero flanked by a bevy of intellectually powerful young women who would look upon me favorably after they'd successfully taken over the world. That first Saturday, I noticed the same woman in both places, a serene-looking person with a resting saint face. I was struck by what I thought was an incredible coincidence—can you even imagine two nice, helpful, white writer ladies who are also interested in deepening their yoga practice?

Well, you don't even have to imagine, because it happened! We were taking part in the same programs at the same time. I introduced myself to her after the mentoring workshop and we chatted about the funny coincidence, which seemed much more remarkable to me than to her. In fact, she seemed borderline weirded out and I regretted slightly that I was the one to notice and say it. I wondered if, just a couple of years into my crash course in American small talk, I had somehow become an advanced practitioner, and opened up a smidge too much without realizing. The saint-faced lady certainly seemed a little put off. Although I kept it light, she seemed pained. Little did she know how valiantly I struggled to resist saying, *And we're both curly girls!* and ask her how often she washed her hair.

After yoga in Brooklyn the following week, it made sense to walk together to the subway to get into the city for the mentoring, so we did. She sighed a tiny bit as we waited for the F train, and I sensed the sigh was not directed solely at the tiresome weekend MTA schedule. The train arrived and we found seats side by side. We sat nicely in our expensive, comfortable clothes and I confessed to her that my heels have never touched the ground in a downward dog. Harmless little opener, I felt. She had her phone out as fast as you could say *So what?* and just as effectively. She did a quick smile and said she was super-busy. You know, with yoga and mentoring and her part-time job. I asked if she was from New York and she said no, and reflexively asked where I was from. Ireland, I told her. She seemed despondent, but soldiered on. "When did you move here?" "Almost two years ago." Suddenly exhausted, she said, "Remind me to ask you about your story when I'm less, like, crazy busy."

That is how it came to pass that instead of some

warm small talk leading to an easy quietness, Warrior One sat beside Warrior Two in tense silence as they both trawled through their phones. My reluctant companion believed that conversation had to be all or nothing, either teetering on ice or plunging into the unknown waters beneath. She didn't know she just had to pull on a pair of skates and twirl around for a while. That elegance was not accessible to her, I thought, as I spied a dog in a bag under the seat opposite us. His little black eyes shone. I get it—words are laughably inadequate when it comes time to express ourselves. My brain is so close to my mouth, yet in the time it takes for a thought to travel between them and become a sentence, the meaning is diluted and fudged to something I don't really mean at all. Be that as it may, words are all we have when it comes to telling someone who we are, so we are duty-bound to at least try. I didn't want a vapid exchange; I'm easily bored and would have made sure to steer away from one. An in-depth conversation wouldn't have been appropriate either, but I had no intention of launching into my whole biography, or asking her to do the same. The perfect in-between connection was small talk, but we missed that connection and now I was just a woman alone on the subway, smiling at a schnauzer.

In Ireland, small talk does not just happen between the newly acquainted. It's the preferred way to communicate with even our nearest and dearest. Admittedly that is annoying if you genuinely want to know how your friend is doing, what they're up to in work, who they're seeing. But just try saying, "How are *you*, though, *really?*" to any Irish person and I'm warning you, you will be decimated. When you've been gone for a while, navigating these ways of communicating can get confusing, and I forget the codes. I forget myself. Or maybe America is rubbing off on me. At Christmas, with three generations of family around the table, I was feeling schmaltzy. I love them so much! I always do, but this time I was flooded with a seasonal type of love, the misguided one that makes you think this time of year is different from others. I was a Christmas cracker, ready to absolutely explode. I remembered an American tradition, one from Thanksgiving, and decided to just go for it. "Why don't we all go around the table, and say what we're thankful for?" The year was a drama-filled one for our family, featuring illness, weddings, babies, as well as the thousands of miles between us. But we'd made it, and now sat around a table laden with delicious food, safe and sound.

But talking about this? No. No way. Looks were exchanged. Those dreadful looks! Those wordless looks! At least seven pairs of eyebrows were raised. "I'll start?" I offered, my voice less sure. "Oh, I forgot we were the Kardashians," muttered one sister, mashing butter into a potato. "Um, I'm grateful for my nieces and nephews . . ."

One sister loudly asked for the Brussels sprouts. I ground to a halt and my mother remarked that Cate Blanchett was really too old to play Maid Marian. Hot and furious tears filled my eyes. How could I be so stupid? I had forgotten myself. One sister noticed me wiping my eyes with a holly-print napkin and saved me further embarrassment by not referring to my tears directly, instead whispering to another sister that I was crying. They glanced at me in astonishment, and averted their eyes. *Ffffuck*, I thought. The least natural and most stupid thing to do is to try to be serious, to force sincerity onto others.

This Anaïs Nin quote that I heard on an Alicia Keys album comes to mind. "And then the day came when the risk it took to remain tight in the bud was more painful than the risk it took to blossom." But Anaïs Nin and Alicia Keys, my dear ladies, aren't you worried that if you don't stay tight in the bud your blossom will be gobbled up by a hungry little billy goat or you'll be shut down on a train or your family will have you committed to a mental hospital? I am. My timing is all off. Throughout the rest of the day, confessional-style, different family members told me in low urgent tones what they were thankful for. "Too late," I said, eyes fixed on *It's a Wonderful Life* as I absolutely shoveled trifle into my mouth. As well as the compulsive need to express oneself as loudly and quickly as possible, there's another great mystery of American life I will never solve, and that is, just why isn't trifle more popular here? Some Americans don't even know what it is. When I meet them for the first time at Christmas parties I explain it's made by lining a bowl with sponge cake soaked in booze, adding some berries for color, then a thick layer of custard, followed by a thicker layer of whipped cream dotted with maraschino cherries. Just a little something light to finish off a rich festive meal. It's small talk, really, something trivial but full of clues, perfectly trifling, perfectly rich.

Wildflowers

I ONCE MADE A PROMISE I couldn't keep. I didn't mean for that to happen, but it did. It wasn't a small one either, but it's like Abraham Lincoln said, "If you're going to make a promise you can't keep, at least make it a big one." Or was that Nixon? I'm not American, so I'm not sure. In any case, I made that big promise to the man sitting opposite me in a chocolate-colored leather booth in a diner just off Union Square. To be fair, I'd just had the rug pulled out from under me by said man and I hadn't even touched my first coffee of the day.

"It's just not working," he said, and gazed at my face for a reaction. I'd heard this from men before, but not in relation to work. Turns out it stung worse when it was. He was talking about the show I'd been developing for the past year, a podcast about immigration. The first season had just aired, we were producing the second, and the show was apparently . . . not working. He was my producer, sitting on the financial side of the podcast boom that was well under way among the many start-up and new media companies sinking money into them. The question was, how to make their money back on a free product? They could sell advertising, but they had to have a hit to make anything like the money they'd put into the production in the first place.

I argued back, at first. "Okay, but immigration is so important right now, Trump was elected on an anti-immigrant ticket and I really feel that if you could just promote it more or—" He interrupted, "Absolutely, and I completely hear you. But the issue here is that the show is just not working." Our show began to air the same week Donald Trump was elected as our next President, and I had a rising sense of panic that we weren't doing enough to amplify the voices of my immigrant guests. I worried that my producers didn't share my urgency, and had said as much in a late-night email the previous evening. "Don't you adore late-night emails?" I'd asked when I saw him in the office that morning. "Not this one," said my producer through a tight smile, and suggested we go for a coffee. Bleary-eyed from lack of sleep and confused as to what was going on, I forgot what Oprah had taught me. I forgot that I should never let them take me to a second location. Even if that location is known for its really good lattes.

He explained to me quickly, with precision, that I was wrong about everything. The show wasn't working. There was no problem with promotion, it's just that the show wasn't working.

"The show is too serious. Nobody wants to listen to a show that feels like taking medicine, they want to listen to a super-fun show!" I had no idea this was coming, and am terrible at any kind of conflict, so I said something mild. "But don't you think it's quite good even if it's not, like, ha-ha funny? And, like, maybe we just need to do more promotion so people can find it? I'm sure they'll like it when they find it." He was insistent. His company had bought my pitch, a comedy podcast about immigration, and where was the comedy? Also, where were the famous people? Surely there were some famous immigrants, and everyone loves celebrities, *that's* how people would discover the show.

"I hope we can work to fix this, or . . ." He spread his hands and gave a quick shrug. The threat was never uttered, but I understood that there would be no third season if I didn't fix it. It was around about then that I flung my principles right out the window, with such little care that they surely crashed among the chess players and Hare Krishnas dotted throughout the park outside. I promised him then. I said, "Okay, cool, this has been great! I'm about to make a trip to the West Coast and do some taping out there, and I promise you that season two is going to be super-fun."

It was definitely true that I was about to make a trip to the West Coast, but the rest, I could not be sure of. Like many Americans and immigrants alike, I'd had a sense of foreboding after the election results were announced. Our new President had made many threats and many promises during his campaign, and we did not yet know which he would act on.

Super-fun. The Muslim ban was about to drop from the White House, stranding immigrants and refugees all over the world. Eight hundred thousand kids who had been granted DACA (deferred action for childhood arrivals) by an executive order created by President Obama, were in danger of becoming deportable when President Trump rescinded the order a few months after this conversation. Neo-Nazis were planning rallies where they would chant, "One people. One nation. End immigration." A month after I made that promise, two Indian immigrants would be shot, one to death, in a Kansas bar by a white supremacist screaming, "Get out of my country." I didn't know all of that then, but even if I did, I probably would have lied, because I just wanted to make the show.

"Awesome." He paid for my untouched coffee and said he would see me back at the office, then flashed a smile as he left. I smiled back, but felt my face crunch into a frown before I realized he was still standing there looking at me. He patted my shoulder, definitely on his way out now. "And get some fish tacos if you visit San Diego, for real. You'll die." "Yummy!" I screamed after him, but I don't think he heard.

Back at the open-plan, glass-walled office full of silent people working in all areas of new media, the only way I could relay a message of this magnitude to my little team sitting right beside me, my junior producer Erika, was on the internal messenger Slack. *We're fucked!* I typed, getting straight to the point. *I promised him a super-fun second season WITH famous people. Do we even have guests in California lined up? Is Javier Bardem an immigrant? Nicole Kidman is, right?* Turns out we didn't have any celebrities booked. We had an Iranian poet and a Romanian cleaning lady. *Both of them are wonderful guests*, Erika typed, *I've done the pre-interviews and their stories are kind of incredible.* I remembered those guest ideas from our pitch meetings weeks earlier, and looked up the notes.

They did have incredible stories. The poet had been flung in jail during the Iranian Revolution, his wife executed a month after that. He'd fled to the U.S. and claimed asylum, raising his son here and finding love once more. Meanwhile, his eyesight had completely failed, he was now blind, but still wrote poetry. The Romanian lady was a lawyer working in the highest offices of Bucharest, the parliament, when she left for Los Angeles for a work opportunity that never came through, and she ended up cleaning houses and selling baseball caps on Santa Monica Boulevard.

These kinds of stories? Not what I'd promised. I bashed my keyboard. *Oh great—like so super-fun.* Erika looked at me across the desk, wide-eyed. I glared back and shrugged, *What?* She stood up and said she was going to Chipotle, did I want anything? I asked her if they did fish tacos, but it turns out they don't, so I got a burrito the size of my forearm to tamp down the stress of the day.

I would usually spend lunchtime teasing Erika about her devotion to The Halal Guys food carts, and she would crack me and our editor Matt up by telling us stories about her doorman dad and what he saw going on around him, or her mom's new business making balloon decorations for christenings and the inevitable pitfalls involved in such an endeavor (e.g., babies are scared of balloons). This lunch was different. It was initially dominated by me freaking out over my upcoming trip, and how I didn't know where to get in touch with Nicole Kidman, and how I could make a meaningful show that told the truth, while also making the show I'd assured my boss I'd make.

Around about then Erika sat back in her chair, folded

her arms, and reminded me of the show's original mission, to amplify voices that were not usually heard: those of immigrants, people like her parents, who had moved from Colombia to escape political violence and had run out of legal status. They were in the shadows until Erika and her twin sister, both U.S. citizens, were able to sponsor them when they turned twenty-one. In the usual stories she told about her parents, she didn't bring that up. Now here she was, going full Queens on me. "Being funny is cool and all, sure, but there were long years we spent frightened of a knock on the door, and I don't think *people* appreciate how messed up that is."

You know how it's rude to eat when someone is relating something sad or frightening to you? Well, I definitely recall not knowing when it was okay to take a bite of my burrito again right after Erika had relived one of the most harrowing moments from all of those years her parents spent undocumented. "Maeve, this shit is real. I was maybe fourteen years old and there was an ICE raid on the floor above us, right in my building, they *took our neighbors*. My mom was just shaking, looking out the peephole, whispering to me, like, *Erika—they're inside—they're inside*."

I flew out the day President Trump was inaugurated and watched the TV screens at Kennedy Airport with my fellow travelers. The rain came down in Washington, D.C., as Trump boomed that he would put America first, that he would end this "American carnage" and protect our borders from "the ravages of other countries." He sounded, to me, like a dark-hearted and frightened old man, but he was our new President, and everyone was listening to him. The only sliver of power I thought I had was to make a podcast about immigration so that people could see how wrong it was to dehumanize others, so people could understand one another better.

A battle began in my brain. It felt grandiose that I, a comic, would deliberately set out to make a self-important piece of work with the goal of changing hearts and minds. Comics taking themselves seriously have always made me laugh. Be that as it may, making a conversation around immigration *super-fun* struck me as inadequate at best, irresponsible at worst. But that was what I had promised to deliver. I reasoned with myself on the flight: I would keep my promise by making something light and fun to listen to. That would please my bosses, a mild-mannered and sweet show that would gradually change the temperature on how immigrants were perceived. By the time I arrived in San Diego that evening, I was determined to be bright and bubbly the next day during my visit to the border wall with Tijuana, and I'd put in some fifteen more requests to interview celebrities in my upcoming L.A. stay.

The next morning, my contact who was taking me to

the border wall, an immigrants' rights activist named Dan, texted to say he was going to the Women's March happening in San Diego before we made our trip, and asked if I'd like to join him. I didn't know what to expect from the Women's March in San Diego. Although San Diego had voted against Trump, I'd heard it was a conservative-leaning town compared to other parts of California, and I didn't know anybody who lived there. On the tram to the city center there were small groups of people clutching signs and posters and wearing pink hats. The posters were funny and scathing and tragic:

THIS PUSSY GRABS BACK;

GIRLS JUST WANNA HAVE FUN-DAMENTAL HUMAN
    RIGHTS;

and

WE ARE A NATION OF IMMIGRANTS

with a hastily scribbled

AND NATIVE PEOPLE

at the bottom.

I met Dan, a soft-spoken man with a black beard, and stood beside him as he wrote his sign in Spanish. Unfamiliar with the city and the plan, I wasn't sure which direction to walk in, but we got buffeted along by little streams of people that turned into rivers and eventually, as rivers always must, into a sea. A sea of thousands and thousands of people who didn't know what else to do except get out onto the street and shout and organize against their own leader, people I'd never met but I shared a cause with now. I checked social media intermittently and saw my friends marching in D.C. and New York and L.A. There were hundreds of marches across the country, with more than four and a half million people taking to the streets. It was an extraordinary feeling, to be this one drop in this ocean of people rolling in waves across the nation, and it was a wild contrast to where I was headed that afternoon, a place that would wash away any chance of me keeping my promise.

Friendship Park is a small park that straddles the U.S. border with Mexico, overlooking the Pacific Ocean. The park was opened by First Lady Pat Nixon on August 18, 1971, as a symbol of friendship between the U.S. and Mexico, where *Thinkprogress* reports that she said, "I hope there won't be a fence here too long." Today, it's the only place along the almost two-thousand-mile border between the countries where people on both sides can meet. When I say meet, I mean they can see each other. Visitors are allowed to see each other every Saturday and Sunday from ten a.m. to two p.m. That's almost all you can do, see each other. You can talk, too, and squeeze the tip of your baby finger through the fence to touch the person on the other side, but that's it.

The park is really just a patch of scrubby land rising

up from the beach. Dan, my guide, visits often, and tries his best to keep some plants alive, but it looks quite bleak on the U.S. side. There are some public toilets now, which he said was a huge improvement for all the families that make the trek there to see loved ones on the other side of the fence. When I say fence, it's not so much a fence as a pair of eighteen-foot-high metal walls constructed by the U.S. government. It's extraordinary to see the walls and know that there was only barbed wire there when First Lady Pat Nixon visited; in fact, she asked that the wire be cut so she could cross into Mexico and say hello to the people there.

Under President Carter, the barbed wire became a chain-link fence, and as immigration policies hardened throughout the years, so did the fence. It became a ten-foot wall of hard wire mesh in 1994. The holes were large enough to hold hands through, but that changed when the federal government reclaimed Friendship Park from the state of California and the George W. Bush administration began the major reinforcement to the border that exists today. In total, the Obama administration deported 2.7 million people, more than the three previous administrations combined, and *The Guardian* newspaper reports that in 2012 alone the U.S. government spent $18 billion on immigration policing—more than it spent on all other federal law enforcement combined.

For a few years after its latest renovation in 2008, the

government closed Friendship Park, only opening it back up to visitors following pressure from churches and humanitarian groups, like Friends of Friendship Park, of which Dan was a member. It's a hugely valuable place, being the only one where you can see your family and friends on the other side, but the walls, vehicles, and guards make the little park look like a militarized zone, with giant metal arms that stretch out over the hills to the east and right along the beach into the sea.

There's an eerie contrast between the beach on the Mexican side of the wall, with picnickers and music and swimming, and the beach on the U.S. side, deserted except for a couple of Border Patrol dune buggies buzzing along the sand, a wheeling seagull above in the sky, and a wheezing Irishwoman trying to catch her breath in the wind as she trudges through the sand. There on that lonely beach, surrounded by armed Border Patrol agents and that eighteen-foot wall, I felt a cold lack of humanity that could not have been more opposed to the jostling purpose of the warm crowd of people I'd experienced that morning.

I met a man at Friendship Park, Enrique Morones, sturdy and smiley, from an organization called Border Angels. I had not planned to meet him, he just happened to be there, bringing around a British journalist and camera crew. It seems to me that not a lot of Americans even know about this park—two friends of mine who grew up in San Diego had never heard of it—but international media have profiled Friendship Park and the people there a number of times. Another irony about the British crew there struck me later, when I realized with dismay the damage Brexit could do to the border in my own country.

I asked Enrique for an interview and, since taping is not allowed inside the park, we sat on the ground outside the gates, sheltering from the wind behind a low wall. Among other advocacy work, Border Angels puts water in the desert to prevent more migrants from dying of thirst. Sometimes their water jugs are slashed by U.S.-based vigilante groups, or rogue elements within the U.S. Border Patrol guards.

In the first seven months of 2017, the International Organization for Migration reported that 232 people died trying to cross the border. They added that this fatality calculation is likely to be an underestimate on their part, because the areas people are crossing are so vast their bodies are often not found. This 2017 number is higher than usual, despite the U.S. Border Patrol reporting that only about half as many migrants were apprehended during border crossings in the first six months of 2016 compared to the first six months of 2017—down from 267,746 people to 140,024 people. The higher death toll may be because, historically, stricter immigration policies in the U.S. have driven people to take more dangerous routes.

There was no doubt in Enrique's mind. "The new President wants to build more walls. That means more death." He described the inauguration day as the saddest day of his life, not just for what was to come, but for the damage already done. "Here's a person that made his entire campaign by first attacking us, attacking Mexicans. Had he started with another group, Jewish people or black people, they would have shut him down, but he started with us, that's how he got his traction." Enrique said that just three months beforehand, two people had attempted to swim across the border from Mexico but had drowned, and their bodies had washed up on the U.S. side of the beach. I knew that this tragedy would not fit on my promised comedy podcast about immigration, and I also knew that I would have to put it in the show. My promise lay snapped at my feet, and I would leave it there, for now.

I wrote quickly in my notebook—*maybe one-off special ep dealing w/border wall and racism then back to superfun*—then went back into the park.

Along the wall there were small clusters of people huddled in to talk to corresponding clusters of people on the other side, more than likely family members. One young man on the U.S. side of wall, who'd taken a bus from L.A., was leaning in close to talk to his mother in Mexico, who'd been deported three years previously because she was undocumented. He was a DACA recipient, so at that time he was safe, but he was unwilling to risk leaving the U.S. even for a trip. His mother had taken a two-hour flight and a five-hour bus trip to see her son at the border. Her hair was in a high bouffant, her makeup bright and pretty, from what I could make out through the tiny gaps in the wall. I spoke with them for a moment, admired her lipstick, and let them get back to their low, rapid conversation.

I could have asked the son to join me outside the gate for a quick interview, but I didn't want to intrude on their limited time together. Another reason I didn't interview him was because I had a lump in my throat just looking at this mother and child, inches away from each other, unable to hug, as the clock ticked on toward two p.m., when the park would close and the border agents would kick the families out of the U.S. side. I felt oddly ashamed leaving the park, nodding to the Border Patrol agent, a handsome Latino man in his thirties with a dapper haircut. Dan led us back across the white sandy beach and the dark muddy trail to the road, and I asked him if he had any fun stories about things that had happened at Friendship Park. I was clutching at straws, imagining perhaps a wonky camaraderie between Border Patrol agents and community groups, or some defiantly witty take on who would pay for the wall. Dan thought about it for a moment before answering, "Not really, it's kind of the most heartbreaking place in America."

Whatever cute idea I had about a show celebrating

this great melting pot of a country, with feel-good stories of fusion food and cosmopolitan couples with bilingual children, seemed hollow to me now. Without dealing with the very real issues of militarized borders and racialized immigration policies, whatever I had to say would be as empty and windy as that beach in San Diego. The next morning, I should have come clean with my producer and accepted whatever was to come. I did not do that. I was still hoping to salvage some part of the promise I'd made, hoping to somehow square the reality with the aspirational, hoping to keep my job.

So I spun what was definitely not a super-fun experience into something I could pitch to my producer, and emailed a breezy note suggesting a short, extra episode about the border. *It won't be as lighthearted as season two is going to be but deffo worth discussion—thanks so much!* I called my junior producer Erika back in New York and asked her if any famous people had agreed to be interviewed, reminding her that my week on the West Coast was running out. Not yet, she told me, but our Romanian cleaning lady in L.A. was getting a little cranky that we had yet to confirm a location and time for her interview. She needed to make sure she could organize time off work, and she had been messed around with by the media before.

I agreed we needed to set a time, and asked Erika if she knew how far away Orange County was from me right now, and in turn how far away Orange County was from L.A. "No clue. But I used to watch *The O.C.* and it seemed like they rarely went into the city." More confused than ever, I hung up and tried to figure out how I was going to get ninety miles up the coast without driving a car. Three buses later I found myself in a Vietnamese sandwich shop, sitting at a table under a mural of James Dean, waiting to interview the owner of the shop and creator of the mural, Lynda Trang Dai. Lynda is known as the Vietnamese Madonna, and she arrived at the table like a whirlwind, a whirlwind with the USA flag painted on her toenails.

Lynda and I had a great interview; she was charming and chatty. She arrived in the U.S. as a three-year-old and adores her life here, a life that's equal parts glamour and hard work. She runs the shop and is a pop star in her spare time, playing shows to huge crowds of people from the 1.2-million-strong Vietnamese-American community, making music videos, and even touring back in Vietnam. Here was someone fun; the interview was the bones of an entertaining episode more in keeping with what I had promised. I should have been relieved—but instead I felt even more confused.

I found it difficult to focus on Lynda's smooth assimilation into U.S. society while still holding on to her own cultural identity, a success story by all accounts, because my mind kept returning again and again to the most heartbreaking place in America. I reminded my-self that immigration adds vast swaths of color to any self-portrait of the U.S., and it incorporates a multitude of tones. There are funny stories and sweet victories in among the struggles and injustices, and surely I could honor those lovely parts too. Perhaps this was the happy mix my producer would accept: a pleasant interview with a charming immigrant, fair ballast to the heavier parts of the story of immigration into the U.S.

After the interview, I stood in the parking lot wait-ing for my taxi when Lynda's father arrived in his pickup truck. A small, wiry man with a shock of gray hair, he reminded me of my own father, particularly when he bent and whipped out a tiny thistle that had just emerged to disrupt the little strip of planting along the front of the restaurant. We talked, taking time to understand each other's accents. In 1977, Dinh got his three chil-dren out of Communist Vietnam on a boat, through a typhoon, and washed up on an island off Hong Kong. "What was that like?" I asked him, as casually as asking someone how their trip to the post office was. He cleared his throat and blinked hard, getting upset.

What did I expect? A confident sound bite, a neat little answer to my question? My question which was ba-sically, *Um, hi, I know I just met you in a parking lot in Orange County, but can you, like, fill me in on the worst mo-ments of your life?* He was gracious enough to keep talking, after steadying himself for a few seconds. He told me he made it to the U.S. as a refugee, built up a construction and landscaping business, and "can't say no" whenever one of his seven grandchildren asks him for anything. I asked him if he had any thoughts on our new President, and he looked down with huge sadness. "I can't bear to look at him." Without this man there would be no Lynda, at least not as the world knew her. Without his stark choice, terrifying journey, and brave actions in escaping with his little girls, followed by a life of hard work, she would not be able to have that super-fun life. And here he was, devastated by the second country in his lifetime to betray him. Omitting his experience from this wider immigration story I'd decided to tell, particularly after he'd shared it with me, after I'd asked him to share it with me, would be a broken promise too.

Checking into my hotel in San Francisco the following day, I noticed a group of people crowded around their phones in the lobby, looking aghast. One woman sat with her hand over her mouth, just staring blankly, her phone on the sofa beside her. I sat next to her, and before I got a chance to ask her what was happening, she asked me, "Did you see what they did? This is not America." It was Executive Order 13769, titled "Protecting the Nation from Foreign Terrorist Entry into the United States." The new administration had suspended all refugees for 120 days pending review, and Syrian refugees indefinitely. Travelers from seven Muslim-majority countries were barred, thousands of visas revoked, and hundreds of people detained at airports.

So the airport was where I needed to be. I checked my recorder batteries in the taxi on the way. As we took the turnoff to SFO, the Lyft driver asked, "Where are you off to?" I replied at once. "Oh, I'm not going anywhere," I told him. "I'm staying right here." It felt like a profound thing to say, but, as is so often the case, it was unhelpful. "Okay. Well, I need to know which terminal, like departures, arrivals, just ballpark where I gotta drop you off." Mortified, I checked Twitter but couldn't get a clear idea of where people were gathering. I asked him to drop me at whichever terminal was closest. The airport felt strange. At first it seemed like business as usual, people milling around, hauling their luggage, chatting on their phones. Then I heard it, a swell of sound coming from downstairs, outside. It was the sound of hundreds of people chanting, and I followed the chanting as it got stronger and stronger, floating up the escalators, booming through the elevators, an irresistible magnet pulling all of us together.

Airport police stood aside as the sidewalk outside the terminal filled with hordes of people holding banners and signs. There were old couples, children, disabled people, of all races and creeds, listening to hurriedly assembled speakers proclaiming the injustice of this ban. More and more people continued to pour in, chanting, "No ban, no wall, sanctuary for all." Lawyers were arriving, worried-looking young women in suit jackets, as was the media, mics charging and laptops plugged into power outlets around the terminal. Cameras crowded around a weeping man as he waited for his pregnant wife. She should have been out by now; he was growing frantic. The crowd soon surged into the terminal, crying, "Let the lawyers in, let the families out." At a certain point I stopped taping and just stood and shouted with the rest of the crowd.

That night, I had to be funny again. I was booked to do some shows at Sketchfest, a comedy festival that takes over the city every January. Jolted into a new realm of awareness, adrenaline high from that day at the airport, I felt very odd preparing to go out with my old routines about dating and bolero cardigans. (Those are two different bits, in case you're wondering; I would never wear a bolero on a date.) I couldn't do that, I had to talk about what was happening to immigrants. I felt bad going onstage in front of an audience who'd bought their tickets weeks in advance and talking about the ban, about how lucky I was to be a European immigrant, to be white, about how bigoted this government was. They had just come for a giggle, to put aside whatever their own troubles were for a bit. They didn't need some newly right-on foreigner telling them her half-formed thoughts. But, thankfully, they were good-natured about it—my real blunder was yet to come.

The comedy festival had a family car waiting to take us back to the hotel, with two rows of seats. After the show, three of us sat in it, one per row, waiting for the headliner, who'd been accosted by fans and was getting her photo taken on the street outside. It's not the greatest feeling in the world, to sit waiting for the star to finish with her public sparkling so you can all go back to the hotel, and the mood was cranky. I read aloud Twitter updates about the ban. "Looks like Iran is retaliating by banning U.S. citizens." The white woman in the seat in front of me rolled her eyes. "Okay, but I mean, it's, like, clearly bad for international relations or whatever, but it's not like I want to visit Iran. Who the fuck wants to go to Iran?" My heart started to beat faster, and I went *in*. I had been to Iran. "Wow, *I* do! I want to go *back* there. It's an incredible place and it smells like bread and roses and there is history and poetry there that Americans don't even get close to. Maybe that's why they're scared of it." She looked sufficiently chastened and I felt quite pleased with myself.

Filled with a newly lit sense of my own importance in this historic moment, I went back to updating the car. "Okay. Okay, so the latest is a judge has ordered a stay on deportations but the DHS was still holding people! Lawyers are trying to get the people out but the cops won't let them! How are they going to defy the courts like this? It's just unprecedented." The black woman in the front seat, quiet until now, heaved a sigh and turned to face me. "Right, unprecedented. Okay. So I guess that whole school segregation thing passed you by, huh?" The thing is, it had. Filled with righteous indignation, I had not thought about how this ugly moment fit into the string of ugly moments that make up U.S. history, something I had been allowed to do because of my privilege. Mind blown open, the ignorance enjoyed by my whiteness exposed for all to see, I sat back. When I glanced at the rearview mirror I met the quizzical eye of the Sikh driver. He shook his head a little, smiling, not unkindly, and turned the radio on.

There was no one moment when I realized that I would have to confront my broken promise of a *super-fun* podcast about immigration, no showdown where I had to face the consequences that would jeopardize my show and career. It seemed that things were happening, both in the news and in my relationship to it, that I was not prepared for. I could not ignore the spasms and pain being felt by the country I lived in. I had to follow the pain, which meant putting aside the jokes and the artifice, for a while at least.

That January in L.A. was full of rain, bringing an end to the drought that had plagued the city for years. Later I'd be back to witness the incredible beauty of the "Super Bloom," when the deserts of Southern California erupted in color. Every spring the annuals that grow in deserts come to life, and because of the drenching rains, that year there was a far greater than usual explosion of wildflowers. The L.A. hills, usually so bare, came alive with vibrant greenery, purple verbena, orange poppies, and beautiful little white and yellow dune primroses.

Getting soaked by the January rain, I didn't know then that an explosion of color and beauty and nature was to come. I'd given up on the idea of finding a celebrity immigrant, and my chances of making a super-fun second season were fading with every encounter. The studio where I was interviewing my final L.A. guest, the Romanian cleaning lady, was difficult to locate. It was in the basement of a university, and the rain came down in stinging sheets as I wandered around the campus looking for the door. My guest had the same problem, and arrived cold and wet and furious.

Liana Ghica has thick black hair and brown eyes that flash with intelligence. She was dressed all in black and was loudly condemning my team in her fabulous Eastern European accent. "You need to be more organized—how am I supposed to find this place? And it is late now. And my shoes, look, they are soaked!" I apologized and showed her that my shoes were soaked through too. She unwrapped her scarf and looked at me. "And for you, it's no problem. For me, I get sick one day, I lose my job. I have no health insurance, okay? It's not the same. You people have messed around with me before." It turned out Liana had spoken to reporters before about her life as an undocumented immigrant, which, aside from being difficult and sometimes painful to discuss, is risky, too. And those journalists were not always respectful of her time and her story. They sometimes ended up cutting it for a "better" one, which felt to her like a betrayal.

I assured her that I would do no such thing. I was *not* looking to exploit her. No, I created this show as a platform for immigrants to tell their own stories. I promised her that we would treat her story—and when I said story, in this case I meant her entire life as an undocumented immigrant—with respect and care. In that moment, I was not thinking about the promise I'd made back in a New York diner to jazz up the show. If I had thought about it, I'd have known I was breaking it once more. Now here I was making yet another promise I was not sure I could keep, telling Liana we would definitely use her story, assuring her it would meet her expectations exactly.

We began taping, and it didn't go very well. Liana was reserved and cautious, and I was hyper-aware that my tone did not match hers, and that jollying her along wasn't going to work out well. The interview revealed the bare bones of Liana's story. She grew up under the Communist authoritarian Nicolae Ceaușescu; she came from an academic family, many of whom fled the regime in the 1980s and were granted asylum in the U.S. She and her parents stayed behind, living in the shadows of a government that was always watching them. She eventually married a neurosurgeon and had a little boy, Vlad. They divorced when Vlad was two. Liana was now a single mother, a label that carried huge stigma with it in 1990s Romania. A teacher at her son's school took her aside and said, "Vlad is exceptionally bright, but it is a pity that being the child of a broken home is and always will be a handicap." This despite the fact that Liana had gone to law school and worked her way to becoming, at twenty-nine, the chief of staff for the deputy of the Department of Justice.

Liana soon secured a job offer with a lobbying firm in Sacramento, and decided to go for it. She entered the U.S. on a visitor's visa a couple of weeks before 9/11, after which the company decided against hiring anyone from outside the U.S. and rescinded their job offer. Her visa expired, but she decided to stay for her son's sake, as well as her own.

We wrapped the interview, and while I felt that hers was a strong voice for the undocumented community, I didn't feel like I knew *her* very well at all. Before she left, she told me that her son, Vlad, a DACA recipient and graduate of UCLA, worked as an immigrants' rights activist, and was helping to host an exhibition the next day. Liana suggested I stop by to meet him, and perhaps have lunch in her house beforehand. So, on my last day in California, fresh out of ideas about how to seduce celebrities onto the show, I happily sat in Liana's spotless and pretty one-bedroom apartment in a neighborhood she called "bad at night." Paintings of Romanian Eastern Orthodox saints and shelves full of tchotchkes watched over us as we ate a delicious chicken stew with a baguette followed by a creamy yogurt cake, made by Liana that morning.

She seemed much happier to be in her own space, a congenial empress welcoming me into her little palace. Liana was less guarded with the mics off, funny and warm, and excited about me meeting Vlad. I suddenly wondered where he slept, and she pointed to a fold-out bed, tucked away now to make room for the table and covered in a rose-colored chenille blanket. I asked her how she would describe their relationship and she said, "He is my rock and my motivation in everything I do."

As soon as we got to the exhibition, organized by the Labor Center in UCLA, I spotted Vlad. He was tall, broad-shouldered, and very white, wearing a blazer and slacks and a smart pair of spectacles. He looked like a Young Republican among the other activist kids, who were predominantly Latinx and Asian and black. He showed me around the exhibition, which was stunning: multimedia and still photos capturing the vibrancy and strength in the undocumented community. There were gorgeous images of graduating college students standing in orange groves, arms flung around their proud parents who worked through the long hot summers in those very groves, their graduation caps decorated with butterflies—the unofficial symbol of the Dreamers—and phrases like GRACIAS MAMI Y PAPI and UNDOCUMENTED AND UNAFRAID.

Much has been written about the Dreamers—the generations of children brought to the U.S. by their parents, who grew up undocumented—and, more often than not, know no other country but the U.S. They are Americans without papers and, while I want to avoid the "good immigrant" narrative, it's impossible not to point out that they really are exceptional people. They were offered a scrap of an opportunity by the Obama administration in the form of DACA and they grabbed it with both hands. As well as working and going to school, they often support their families, not just financially but with paperwork, language translation, and deciphering other codes of life in the U.S. that are unfamiliar to their parents. The larger story of the Dreamers is a feel-good story, beloved by many a media outlet. But there is a flip side to that level of perfection, and in my new wide-awake state I couldn't help but ask about it.

I asked Vlad about this pressure, to be good, to be perfect. He said that as a child he was simply in survivor mode. "The focus was on doing well at school, that was my train of thought for a long time, doing what I could to prove we deserved to be here." He started working after school as soon as he could, painting houses, dog-sitting, tutoring, and doing more than five hundred hours of voluntary community work in high school, determined to make the case that he and his mother belonged here in the U.S. Now, at twenty-four, he has a more measured view. "It's ridiculous that people have to earn their humanity in this country. But it's a reality; many folks are fighting to prove themselves." He and the other activists were preparing for the worst—that is, the end of DACA.

When the DACA option first became available, it took Vlad almost a year to convince his mother that he should sign up for it. Liana did not trust the government not to use the information provided by the recipients against them and their families, particularly when a new administration came along. Now, of course, we know she was right to be wary. But even as he argued for it back then, Vlad had reservations about DACA and the way it separated people into categories—kids from their parents, the worthy from the unworthy. "I look back on it and realize there is a bigger systemic issue at play, and it strikes me as backward that there is less value on the life of my mother. I'm elevated because of my education, and she is ignored."

There was so much consideration in everything he

said, a caution many undocumented people, even those with DACA, have no choice but to practice. They cannot be flip. This is not to say they can't be joyful, or funny, or smart-mouthed. It's just that, because of their precarity in the U.S., they are deadly serious about it. I asked what it was like growing up with Liana, and he said he felt that they were a little team, despite the fact that he spent a lot of time alone as she worked two or even three jobs. He also said she was relentless in making sure he got his education. I laughed a little and said I could imagine that—after all, she is so fierce. "That's who she has had to be—as much as that is a beautiful quality, I think we can't overlook the fact that, how do you put it . . .?" He thought for a second before continuing. "Forging steel requires a lot of hammering, a lot of heat, and a lot of pressure. It's admirable, but it means people have scars and they've been through a lot."

I've long been fascinated by the multiverse theory, in which physicists examine the possibility of a cosmos in which there are multiple universes. Each alternate universe carries its own different version of reality. Rarely, if ever, do we get a glimpse of the shape our own lives may take in the multiverse. That evening at the exhibition in L.A., I met a woman who may well have been Liana, existing in another universe in the same cosmos, living a life that veered close to Liana's until it took a few small turns in another direction and emerged wholly different.

Like Liana, Marina Andrei is a small woman, with thick black hair and eyes that flash with intelligence. She grew up in Romania and went to the same university and the same law school in Bucharest as Liana. They had the same professors, and ambitions, and both have one child. But their universes diverged at some crucial moments; Marina has a happy marriage to a Romanian husband who supported her when they moved to California and she studied for the bar exam there. She is now an immigration attorney in L.A., with her own practice, and a sharp sense of how much chance is involved in all of our lives.

Marina did not know Liana until she moved to L.A., and the ebb and flow of their parallel lives is something she feels keenly: "Knowing the potential she has, it breaks my heart thinking that she doesn't have the same opportunities I did." As we stood in a doorway, holding little warm glasses of sparkling water, Marina told me of the dangers faced by Liana and her other undocumented friends and clients. "You don't have an identity, tomorrow someone might knock on your door and you're gone." It struck me then how brave Liana was to tell her story publicly, as I'd asked her to. The dangers are so great when you are undocumented; I don't believe I had appreciated the risk she was taking until that moment. I asked Marina how it felt to look out from her own neatly ordered universe, with little piles of paperwork all in place, over to Liana's universe, one swirling with uncertainty. Her throat caught. "I have no words. She poured everything she had into her relationship with her son. I look at her and I think that raising her son the way she did, and preparing him for this battle, that is her victory."

Liana's story was my story, and it wasn't one that I could dress up in a neat little narrative, let alone tie with a *super-fun* ribbon. Her story was the one I cared about now, the one I wanted to share and amplify as my own small way of opposing the wrongdoings forever unfolding here in the U.S. I looked at Liana, posing for a photo with other parents of Dreamers, physically embracing her undocumented community, face flushed with pride. She was not a cleaning lady, a former lawyer, a devoted mother, an undocumented immigrant. She was the super-bloom.

Back in New York, there was no good way to dress up my broken promise. There was no super-fun show with celebrities and jokes. Reviewing my material, I could see there was a series of voices, real and urgent, bursting out with stories that I knew were not told enough. The ice-cold gap between reality and entertainment was not one I could bridge. Back at the office, my producer had not given up. He was upbeat that now, with the travel ban in the news, there was a possibility of booking one of my high-profile comedian friends to talk about Syria, or maybe getting a YouTuber with over a million followers to do a spot on the podcast—that way we could maybe get a shout-out in one of his videos. I couldn't even pretend that I thought this might work. I said it wasn't possible, and explained who I had lined up in the coming weeks: an actual Syrian asylum-seeker, a luggage salesman, devoted father, a man desperately trying to quit smoking but worried about putting on weight if he succeeded.

Erika and I moved out of the office and into a co-working space in Brooklyn. When it came to the second series, I couldn't do what I'd promised, and when I explained why, over an excruciating conference call made from the rented boardroom, my producer didn't buy it. Literally, he didn't buy it. The podcast was not commissioned again. I understood. I had let him down. We released an extra episode covering the border wall and the executive order, but our second-season order was cut by four, which meant four fewer episodes than we had originally planned. I never got to broadcast Liana's story. I had let her down too. I couldn't use the interviews with Vlad and the other young DACA kids. I had let them down as well, just as the country was about to, only in a far more resounding way, by revoking legal status for almost a million of them.

I comforted myself with the idea that perhaps, out in the multiverse, there is another hapless podcaster, one who somehow manages to get it together in time to marry Oscar Isaac so that together they can make an absolutely hilarious show about immigration and it's a hit and the producer makes his money back and all Americans wake up and begin to treat all immigrants with some measure of humanity and dignity. In the meantime, here in my actual universe, I had to call Liana and explain what had happened. Naturally, I dreaded the call, and feared the worst. I thought she would feel betrayed, and be angry at me for wasting her time, and her son's time, and for not understanding how important it was to speak up for people who cannot speak up for themselves. Not so. "I understand," she said. "And I believe that you can find some other way to tell our story, can't you?" I hadn't thought of that. Instantly, out tripped a line. "I will try," I told her before I hung up, but it wasn't a line, actually. It was a promise I knew I would not let myself break.

Other People's Children

I DON'T HAVE ANY CHILDREN of my own, at least, none that I know of. This fact, whenever I care to think about it, kind of amazes me. Its not that I want a child, or planned for one, it's just that I'm from a country with the consistently highest birth rate in Europe and the actual pet name "Mother Ireland." Abortion is illegal in Ireland, and when I was a teenager there was a doctor in the town I grew up in who refused teenagers the contraceptive pill on the grounds of his own religious beliefs. I'm one of eight children, born to parents who have fostered over a dozen more children, including three little sweethearts who live with them still. I'm the only one of my group of school friends not to have children; in fact, they have at least two each.

So, I don't have any children of my own. I do, however, have a number of other peoples' children who have
crawled, toddled, and roller-skated their way into my
life. I have all these nieces, four of them, and if I could,
I would profile each one of them the way those slavering
pop culture writers do with celebrities. You know, "Hazel sits on the patio telling us about her life, her chubby,
tanned hands flying through the air as she babbles, before hoisting herself up onto the table and laughing as
she sips hot chocolate from a puddle she has spilled just
moments before. She's pretending to be a dog now. It's
not hard to see why everyone is besotted with this toddler." That is the kind of news I want to hear, but it
seems that unless a person is related to me, it's very difficult to convince them to even spend ten minutes looking at a series of photos of my nieces.

Some of my pregnant or trying-to-get-pregnant
friends allow the slideshow, but, come to think if it, they
never request it. Usually I have to seize the opportunity
that happens the moment after someone shows me a
photo of their own children. *Uh-huh*, I say, looking at
the infant for the obligatory twenty seconds, *very cute/
alert/healthy*, and then I absolutely bombard them with
photos and videos of my nieces at various stages of their
lives. If they are not sufficiently intrigued, and they
never are, I make a scene. *You people don't seem to appreciate just how astounding it is that just a couple of years ago*

*these little girls didn't even exist. And now I have actually
THREE two-year-old nieces!*

There really should be a TV show, a half-hour comedy drama where I and these baby girls all somehow end
up living together in a loft apartment. Not for some
tragic reason, like death or abandonment, maybe just
because my sisters end up in maximum-security prison
or something. Anyway, the working title is *Aunt You
Glad I'm Not Your Mother?* And it would be a gentle,
apolitical show where my nieces (played by themselves)
would lounge around making tea in tiny kitchens and
building castles in a sand pit while I (played by me)
panic and try to maintain a romantic life and have a lot
of groceries to buy.

The story lines would be quite mild, the cliff-hangers
not too steep, just things like, "Will Sadie find her
soother in time for bed?" The art director could build
out the sets to look bigger as the girls get taller, so they
will always look small and cute. To be frank, a huge and
possibly odd part of me wants to bonsai these little girls,
to keep them exactly the way they are. They already
have a number of brilliant character traits: they are as-
sertive, hilarious, and gentle. They are so intensely vulnerable, small little scraps who cannot fully express
themselves, but at the same time they're crazily determined to thrive, grabbing everything they can reach,
relentlessly curious about the world. Their characters are

already well developed. Hazel has decided against me. I'm having dinner in her house and she looks at me over the rim of her sippy cup and whispers, "Go. Home." I ask her, feigning sadness, "Should I go home? Down to Nana's house?" She nods, watching me carefully. Sadie is a doll come to life, straight out of the 1950s with a head full of curls and a shy little smile. When things get too hectic for her, she pretends to be asleep. Nora has a Filipino accent, because all of her nursery staff in Dubai, where she lives, are from the Philippines. Her games consist mainly of tea parties with her dolls where she urges the dolls to "be careful" in her Filipino accent. I need to see to it that these girls keep their strength up, that they never go quiet, and, when they need to, that they always put up a fight.

I have another niece too, my eldest niece, and she is five. Like any person, she is many things, but chief among them she is competitive and fierce and funny. She strides through her day on long spindly legs, hazel eyes sparking as she invents games and organizes other children, focusing as she clambers and scrapes her tiny self to the top of a twelve-foot climbing frame until she is waving and hooting from the top. To watch her learning how to read and see how determined she is to master writing, and, when she finally manages a word, to hear her telling her mother, "You know, writing's actually *really* easy"? Well, it's enough to blow your heart open.

Therein lies the problem: my heart can't handle these girls. Typical, really, it's the most unreliable of all my organs. My stomach can handle anything, believe me. My kidneys give me no trouble, and my brain provides just enough clear spells to get by. It's my heart that goes out to people, gets full up, skips a beat, stops. It's my heart that jumps up into my throat and drops down, too far down to carry on without it. To keep my heart intact, I must keep these little girls intact. It's a selfish kind of love I have for them, I think, one that instinctively knows protecting them from harm protects me from harm. Perhaps that is what's behind my wish to desert my current life and devote a new one to them. And since the TV show is unlikely because the lame-stream media is too lily-livered to cast three unknown babies as leads in a multimillion-dollar series, and my sisters will more than likely stay out of prison, I have another scenario in mind that would allow me to spend more time with the girls.

I'd like to shadow them daily, in a pantsuit, some kind of unconventional bodyguard, with my thin lips pursed. From day one I'd be there, telling the midwife to take it easy, correcting people who failed to support their little wobbly heads. "Is she the . . . governess?" people would ask. "No, no," I would laugh, then just as quickly I'd stop laughing and say, "I'm the aunt." As they grew into toddlers I'd crouch behind them on the swing set, aware of but not actively listening to the current playground gossip. If it's about one of my nieces, I'd tower over whoever was saying it and ask in a menacing voice, "What was that, Becca?" I'd hover in class, and pinch any children who tried to distract them. The teachers would be fine with my presence, because teachers are almost always aunts too.

My nieces' teenage years would see an acceleration in my work. I would accompany them to parties, and if they faltered I'd whisper to them how cool they are, how special, how worth knowing. When they had something to say I'd urge them on "louder, again." I'd tell them absolutely everything they needed to know: how to squeeze blackheads without leaving a scar, that Raymond Carver doesn't matter as much as Nina Simone, that the sooner they figure out a way to make their words match their thoughts, the better. They would grow used to me always being there, having never known any different. At summer camp, if anyone asked who that brown-haired frowning woman was, the one always at their shoulder, they'd have to think for a second before saying, "Oh. That's my aunt."

Ideally, every girl would have an aunt, keeping an eye on things, stepping in when needed. It's practically impossible to see the actual structures in which our lives are shaped. There are codes and norms that are so codified and so normalized that they create a veil of order that we don't think about, because we can't see it. I sense that the order, at this time in the world, is that women are not as valuable as men. We are treated, in a million ways, as beings worth less than men. If I'm wrong about that, great. If not, then I must be an aunt, and there must be many more like me. Our aunt ranks will be made up of women who have somehow managed to wrench off that veil placed so craftily on us as we grew up, obstructing our view of the truth, which is that women are just as valid and important and human as men.

Perhaps it's impossible to fully pull that veil off, but those of us who have worn it for long enough that it has grown transparent in patches and loose at the ends, allowing glimpses of truth and rushes of oxygen, at least we can step up. We will be an army of women, there to protect these girls and claim back their land. Our recruits will come from all around. Aunts can be mothers too. And, actually, boys can be nieces. You don't even need to be related to a niece to be her aunt, did you know that? Nieces are everywhere and the aunt ranks are made up of any woman who can guide a girl to safety.

The reasons I don't actually do this protective work full-time are simple, but painful to accept. Firstly, I haven't been able to keep me or my sisters and friends safe from this world of ours, from this dangerous order, so I still have much to learn. Secondly, my overwhelming wish for these girls is autonomy. And how can they really achieve that if I am always there, grimacing at every slight, fingers hovering over my throwing stars, ready to defend them? I don't want anybody to control them, not even me. Independence is a muscle, one that needs to be stretched and challenged and broken down a little in order to get good and strong. I understand that. I won't cast this creeping shadow of caution over their brightness. I will fight the urge to tell them to slow down. I will absolutely stand guard, but from a distance. I want them to be fearless, so I won't tell them to be careful.

I do keep up my aunt work part-time. When I first moved to the U.S. and money and opportunities were scarce on the ground, my roommate asked me if I wanted to do a babysitting job she couldn't make it to. She hadn't met the family, but the mother of two girls had seen a sign she'd posted in a coffee shop and contacted her, asking for after-school help twice a week. I went to meet the family, high up in a beautiful apartment building overlooking Prospect Park in Brooklyn, where they lived on an entire floor.

The little girls, eight and ten at the time, were funny and inquisitive and clever. They had some questions for me, like how many brothers and sisters do I have, and what word do I use for fart. I told them, seven and buzzer. That seemed to do the trick, and the following week I stood outside their school gates, looking for one head of strawberry blond curls and one chestnut bob among the backpacks and babysitters and stay-at-home dads. We meandered back to their house via a bagel detour, where they showed me a cool game that I think is called "Wave." You basically sit in the safety of the bagel shop, then you wave, very earnestly, at a stranger through the window. If the stranger waves back, which they often do, looking quite baffled, you win.

That afternoon was the most fun I'd had in weeks, and completely different from the babysitting experiences I'd had as a teenager. Back then, my sisters and I had a cottage industry going on. As each of us turned fourteen, we gradually began to babysit everyone in our neighborhood. Like any good service providers, we did not take it personally if someone specifically asked for me, or Lilly, or Ettie. More often, people would call the house and ask for "one of the girls" and we would argue about who should take the gig. Factors to consider included the number and temperament of the children in question, the number and quality of TV stations available, but mainly, of course, the number and quality, or lack thereof, of the snacks at our disposal. I really liked the Sullivan house because they had cheap, plentiful snack food, like these pickled-onion-flavored chips called Meanies that my mother didn't allow in our house.

I wonder now at the wisdom of handing over responsibility for your children to a person so young their own mother still controls their snack choices, but I didn't ask any questions at the time. I was just so pleased to be getting the equivalent of three dollars an hour, and I certainly didn't have anything else going on during my Saturday nights. We were responsible girls, well used to children, having grown up with a number of younger sisters ourselves, but that doesn't cancel the fact that I was usually just a few years older than the children I babysat. One time, when I went to one of my regular jobs, the family's thirteen-year-old cousin was staying for the weekend. I was a year older than her, but I wasn't sure if she knew that. We sat together watching *Friends* on television until nine o'clock, when I told her to go to bed and go straight to sleep.

And now, almost twenty years later, I found myself babysitting again. That only struck me as odd the second week of my new job, as I waited outside the girls' school. My mind began to race. *How am I doing this?* I had my own TV show in Ireland. I had a book published. Yet here I was, happily waiting to pick up a couple of kids at the school gates. I'd been looking forward to seeing them all day. Was this what I wanted? Or was it just an inevitability I could not run from? I wondered if I was like those badgers that blindly walk the same path as their ancestors, regardless of the danger, regardless of the busy roads built over those paths that will inevitably lead to their annihilation.

I thought about my eldest sister Ettie, working for UNICEF in Jordan, looking after Syrian refugee children; my mother in Ireland, still fostering children after her own have grown; little Nora's Filipino kindergarten teachers; and these other babysitters standing beside me at the gates, older West Indian women waiting for their little white charges. How much agency did each one of us have, when it came down to it? I had more than most, I'm sure, but here I was, one more woman taking care of children. It was a strange feeling, a mixture of pride at being part of this nurturing collective, sadness that I was reverting to type, and confusion over what was deliberate on my part, and where the invisible line lay. Then Avra appeared, her beautiful little face shining up at me, and Dahlia too, beaming as she thumped me in the side before I got a chance to duck, and we went to get bagels and talk about the world.

The Golden Record

I AM ADDICTED TO INSTAGRAM, specifically Instagram Stories. If you don't know what I'm talking about, please bear with me; for your understanding of what follows, it's not necessary to share my addiction. In fact, it could well be better if you don't, for your own sake. Or perhaps not. Shall we see? Stories is a feature on Instagram that successfully mimics Snapchat, where you can post as many videos and photos as you like, with any number of filters, stickers, and text, and it doesn't show up on your main feed. So, as Instagram says, "You don't have to worry about over-posting." A Story lasts twenty-four hours, then it disappears forever.

In August, I visited Ireland for my sister's wedding. In the run-up to it, my father celebrated his birthday and I was playing a comedy festival in Dublin. Lovely occasions, all: celebrations, family time, and reliving memories of home. Before I left for Dublin, I was extremely excited about making the trip. Not because of homesickness, or a love of work, or even the chance to escape the sticky heat of a New York summer. All I could think about was the content.

I caught myself grinning in bed one night, imagining the quality and quantity of content those occasions would generate. I suddenly felt grotesque, focusing so hard on the material I could glean for social media from what should really be a lovely private vacation. My grin dropped, until a moment later when I successfully brushed my qualms aside by picturing toddlers on bouncy castles. Adorable! I could film them in "rewind" mode, making them look like superheroes with pigtails! And it would be good for showing off my work stuff too, the festival shots. I envisioned the hyped crowds of people waving in sequence as I snapped a photo of them from the stage. I'd look like a stadium performer, the Springsteen of hesitant observational comedy.

All of that would come along and be picked clean and fed to my phone even before the big day itself, and there would definitely be stunning shots from that, I mean, my wedding day, my big day, the day I'd always dreamed of! Excuse me, I beg your pardon, I meant to say my *sister's* big day. Either way, there would be tearful speeches, heavenly food and sweet little flower girls.

And I was determined that there would be at least one glorious image of me on the wedding day itself, in my wedding dress, as in the floaty pale pink dress I was wearing for the wedding, looking adorable and ephemeral, like a healthy fairy. The dress was actually a little too close to my skin tone for comfort, but I knew I could play with the contrast and filters before I posted it. I knew I could make it all look perfect.

Perfection, when contrived, is laughable. Instagram is easy to dismiss for the way it flattens and fluffs. I'm happy to put up with accusations of vanity, though, to put something beautiful out there in the ether. Besides, I go for perfection in my posts, fun in my Stories, and that's my clunky motto. Perhaps because they disappear, the Stories people post tend to be more spontaneous, more silly, and definitely more enthralling than regular videos. There's a comedian I know a little, and every day I see their little Mexican hairless dog trembling in anticipation of a walk; I watch Chance the Rapper's baby girl learn to count; and I see what my sister Lilly is making for lunch. Stories are hypnotic, endless tiny glimpses into peoples' homes and heads. To stitch them all together into one big quilt to wrap myself in would surely answer every question I have about who we are and why we're here. *This is what I've been looking for*, I think, rapt, as I lie dead-still in my bed, tapping the snooze button on my alarm for the fourth time that morning.

I'm cautious of this addiction, and of this belief that a new piece of technology can allow me into the secret lives of others, because I've fallen in love like this before only to see it all fall to pieces. For a brief few weeks during a comedy festival in Melbourne in 2010, I got completely hooked on Chatroulette. Still in its first year, this chat website randomly connected users to each other so they could chat over video. The Russian teenager who created it, Andrey Ternovskiy, named it Chatroulette because of that scene in *The Deer Hunter*, where prisoners of war are forced to play Russian roulette. That note should probably have signaled how it would all end up, a game of chance with terrible consequences. In this case, while I never blew my head off, I certainly saw many, many headless men masturbating.

But there was a sweet spot just before that happened that lasted at least those few weeks I spent captivated in a Melbourne hotel room, flashing through portals into other worlds. When people who didn't share a language were connected, we could still smile and wave or conduct impromptu puppet shows. I was randomly connected to a German couple having a dance party with their friends, a teenager in Florida who wanted to talk about legal drinking ages, and an architect in Israel who carried his laptop outside to his veranda so we could see the sunset together. It felt like a real human connection, albeit through code.

Soon enough, though, the curious ones, us chatty ones interested in connecting, we were outnumbered. Click after click became dick after dick. Like most of the Internet, Chatroulette soon got overwhelmed by all the dicks, and women, who were less likely to venture on there in the first place, almost completely stopped visiting. Instagram feels much safer, although of course there's a price to pay for that, with their standards that ban female nipples and their ever-increasing number of advertisers barreling through my feed. For now, Instagram and Stories have restored for me a place to join in, to span time and geography and connect with others as we all express ourselves in whichever way we see fit, as long as we don't show our nipples.

Before I left, my therapist asked me how I planned to deal with all the feelings a trip to Ireland evokes in me. A visit home typically presents me with a real smorgasbord of emotions. I feel guilt for leaving, regret at old failures there, joy at being in a place so familiar, and love for my people and my misty little country. These feelings generally mix in together to create some kind of phantasm that blurs up on me and swallows me whole at the arrivals gate in Dublin Airport. I answered my therapist immediately. "Ummm, maybe I will just stack those feelings up and organize them when I'm back?" We smiled and bowed at each other slightly, as we always do when I make some kind of corny joke to buy time, and I sighed. "I suppose I'll steer clear of alcohol and I'll write down my feelings and express myself the best I can in the moment I'm feeling something." Expressing my feelings in the moment as best I could? I didn't know it then, but Instagram helped me to do just that.

I walked through the streets of Dublin, feeling like a weird ghost myself, because me and those streets, we know each other well, but I'm not there anymore. I lived there, in five different homes, for twelve years. Now I don't have a home there. The redbrick buildings on South Great Georges Street are still standing; the unchanged smell of peeled eggs and coffee wafts out of Simon's Place, where I used to sit with my first boyfriend; the national broadcaster still plays the Angelus bells at midday; and the same man with bright blue eyes sits begging on Wicklow Street. There should be a word for what feels like déjà vu but for when you actually have experienced the situation before. Memory isn't the right one. Memories are what I have when I'm away. There is something physical that happens, something more than a memory that crowds in when I'm back there again. I try to document it. I capture the sound of the church bells, the metallic blue of the River Liffey, and the steam from the hot cup of tea I pour on my first morning back, and I put them all on my Instagram Story. I'm saying, *Can you see this? All of this is still here, and now I am back here too.*

The best functions of this feature are the ones that

are missing. There are no likes and no shares—the usual call-and-response reward system that goes with most forms of social media is gone. When I use Stories, I feel less like those laboratory rats who keep pressing a button for more cocaine. Which is nice. I wonder how much longer the feature will last; it's existed since August 2016 and has grown to over 250 million users in a year. It is increasingly filling up with advertisements that snap me out of my reverie as I watch other peoples' Stories, causing me to huffily close the app altogether.

Of course, I open it again soon after. I scroll through my friends' Stories back in New York. There was a double rainbow in Williamsburg and most of them captured it. I love to think of them all taking a second to look up and do that. The guy I'd just started dating had a Story up: pretty standard fare of trees swaying and his cat looking pissed off with a cone around her neck. He must have gotten her spayed, praise be. For a second I'm back on his bed, listening as he explains, haltingly, that she gets so horny, and loud about it, he has to rock her hips to "calm her down." And in that second I'm horrified and impressed all over again at this man who loves his cat so much he'll help her masturbate. I wonder idly if he bothers to check who has watched his Story. I often check, although when over a thousand people have, it's hard to keep track. The ability to see a list of names of people who have watched your stories is an intriguing feature. It is very satisfying for the imaginative among us—I know that my busy little brain whirs to make sense of it all. Why is he watching, is she showing someone else, what will they all think of me now? Sometimes, before I post, I need to stop and check: Are these thirst traps? Some photos, some videos, am I hoping they will set in motion some kind of tryst, like perhaps I'm "tryna fuck," as my young friends would say? Yes, sometimes, but mostly this is bigger than some low-level neediness. I am sending these out to the world, anyone, anyone, anyone there? These images are me trying to say, to anyone who cares to look, *this is what it's like, this is who I am.*

I do my work in Dublin, performing at a comedy festival and doing radio interviews to promote the shows. The conversations I have, both on and off stage, are easy and feel natural on all sides. I find I can say less in Ireland and express more; the fluency I'm missing when I'm away comes straight back into my mouth, and it's a joy. I begin taping snippets of conversations, with taxi drivers and waitresses and comedians, and putting them on Stories. I'm sitting with old friends drinking wine after a show and I realize how much I miss them. I begin to miss them again even though they're right here right now, talking to me. I whip out my phone and make a quick Story, and the sad spell is broken. I have reset the tone. Somehow, by leaving the moment, I've jolted myself back into the moment.

In physics, the observer effect is the fact that observing, or measuring, a situation or phenomenon necessarily changes that phenomenon. Light itself is powerful enough to alter what is going on. Say, for example, that phenomenon is a table full of friends who live far away from each other. This observer effect is caused by an instrument used to observe or measure that table full of friends, thereby transforming the state of that table of friends. The instrument in this case was my smartphone, halting proceedings for a few seconds, capturing and sending our likenesses out into the world. The observer effect is a result of the measurement process because the tools we use to measure are cumbersome on a quantum level, and I wonder if my friends would be unaffected if they didn't see the camera or hear me bellow at them to strike a pose. Or maybe in this case the observing process is some proof of quantum entanglement, that the photons zipping around between people and phones are all jumbled up together. Is my phone a part of me, and vice versa?

Whatever the science, I sense that depicting reality gives me a break from reality. After Dublin, I go back to my hometown of Cobh. Walking into the kitchen in my family home from the clear cool air outside is an intense experience for the senses. There are fifteen voices all speaking at once, telling each other where to sit and what to eat, the smells from the stove of a huge pot of curry, and, of course, a huge pot of new potatoes, the steam from which fogs up the windows. I step carefully over a baby staring up at me from an unexpected spot on the floor to get to my chair, which my father has just placed beside his.

This scene in the kitchen impacts more than my senses, of course; it goes into and among whatever it is behind the senses and throughout them, the extra perceptions every individual feels. In my case, at that lunch, it was delight at the prospect of this gathering and also some nervousness, some small anxiety I couldn't name. To manage it, to lessen the impact, I would record it, just for ten seconds, a short sip of oxygen before I went back under. In that case, my phone certainly pulled me out of the moment, but sometimes I need that or I go too far in and get lost.

On my father's birthday, he's helping to set up a bouncy castle for the grandchildren. He struggles under the weight of the pump, as I stand close by, empty-handed except for my phone, trying to get a Boomerang of him staggering. I wander off, and get annoyed at my parents' little wire-haired Jack Russell, Lacey, for not doing her tricks in the order I want them for my story, so I'm saving the content and rearranging it. "Paw then dead, Lacey, paw *then* dead." Lacey is confused and tired. I'm treating her like Hitchcock treated his blondes.

Meanwhile, my mother, whom I miss like crazy when I'm five thousand miles away, calls my name and

I'm annoyed that she has disturbed me. She is in the kitchen trying to make potato salad for the twenty people coming for lunch. She asks me in to help with the peeling and I shout back, "I'll be there in a second, I'm just finishing a work email." I'm ignoring my own mother, who asks for so little, so I can have more time to watch Lizzo and her band of plus-sized babes shake their butts on a tour bus. I get such a kick out of Lizzo's Stories! Ten minutes pass in a heartbeat, and the potatoes are peeled by the time I look up.

I could watch other people's Stories all day long. Perhaps because they disappear, people are less guarded in their Instagram Stories. They film themselves on the toilet, in their beds, cooking dinner. Not all at the same time, of course. I love this peeping, because I'm nosy and it's usually really difficult to see inside peoples' homes unless you befriend them, or sleep with them, or have children who visit them so that when you collect those children you can strain your neck on their porch, trying to see what type of chairs they have. I snoop happily, globally. I check in on a jazz musician I met once, he's having a lovely time hiking in Oregon. I see my sister is getting coffee with her old boss, and wonder why that is. SZA posts a photo of someone's tattooed hand on her shoulder, whose is it? While I take all these little trips into other peoples' worlds, my body lies inert, slumped on an office chair in a hot little room. Sometimes the app keeps an image of my unaware face that flashes up, and when I log back in I see a digital Turin shroud, somehow both slack-jawed and anxious.

As well as poking around in other peoples' lives, I have this busy little mind that is preoccupied with reaching out, explaining, and tweaking whatever I see before me. I am intent on communicating my experience. I make my own Story, chatting into the camera, resisting the urge to watch it back, trying very hard and very consciously to be unselfconscious. I have always felt a longing to be heard and seen and understood. If I was a cavewoman I'd certainly be the one back in the cave during the elk hunts, with a worried face, frantically using bison blood and blueberries on the walls to explain how I didn't like loud chewing sounds and I love music and I don't think I want children because you should only have them if you really want them and I just don't feel that strongly about it but all the same I'd like you to know that. This impulse to share, possibly to overshare, is easy to scoff at. Add to that how the will to communicate online so often gets mixed up in the aesthetics, with Instagram so full of images, photos, and videos, and I can understand why it is much-derided, and even how it's accused of being an empty vessel with a pretty exterior.

It's easy to dismiss Instagram as trifling and trite, but I see this small way of communicating as potentially very powerful. The twin *Voyager 1* and *2* spacecraft launched in 1977. They are small crafts, just the size of a car. Today, *Voyager 1*, the faster of the two, is 11.7 billion miles away from us, the farthest from Earth of any man-made object ever. In 2012, *Voyager 1* left the heliosphere and entered interstellar space, which is where Sandra Bullock went in the movie *Interstellar*; it has never been visited by a person in real life, and remains the kingdom of the stars. Both spaceships have sent brand-new information back to Earth via radio waves, revealing that the moons orbiting Jupiter are worlds in their own right, and showing us how Saturn's rings have intricate weaves, and Earth is just a pale blue dot in the hugeness of the cosmos.

I love to think of those little spaceships going about their business, hurtling through space, because they're not just reporting back to us, they also have a message to share. Each craft carries a copy of the "Golden Record"— an actual phonograph record full of the sounds and sights of Earth. There are taped greetings in fifty-five languages, an hour and a half of music from all around the world, and 115 analog-encoded photographs showing a selection of just what it is we get up to down here. Etched on the cover there's a diagram with instructions on how to play the record and see the images and an inscription that says "To the makers of music—all worlds, all times" hand-etched on its surface. The thinking was, I suppose, that if any alien is clever enough to catch the spacecraft, it would be well able to decipher the record too. The record is a time capsule, the best we could come up with to introduce ourselves, to say, "Hello, this is what you should know about us." More specifically, a woman speaking the Chinese dialect of Amoy says, "Friends of space, how are you all? Have you eaten yet? Come visit us if you have time."

Between you and me, and I may sound like some kind of drunk empress here, but I have much more grandiose hopes for my Instagram feed than a mere thirst trap, or some public way to demonstrate status. On a good day, this is how I see it. If the Internet is space, then my iPhone is *Voyager 1* and Instagram is my Golden Record. Coincidentally, the entire computing power that has navigated *Voyager 1* over its 11.7-billion-mile journey from Earth can now be found inside an iPhone. I've got the same capability as *Voyager 1* in the room next to me right now. It's off, because I can't write when it's on, because I get too distracted by social media and the time slips away, so I dole it out in parcels between writing time. President Jimmy Carter said of the Golden Record, "This is a present from a small, distant world, a token of our sounds, our science, our images, our music, our thoughts, and our feelings. We are attempting to survive our time so we may live into yours." And, you see, I am a small, distant world too, and my Instagram is a token of my sounds, my science, my images, my music, my thoughts, and my feelings. I am attempting to survive my time so I may live into yours.

The greatest scientific and creative minds in the U.S., led by Carl Sagan, were at work on the record long before I was even born. These great minds did not scoff at the task. They understood the importance of communicating what they were about, they tried to encapsulate their world as succinctly and elegantly as possible. Images on the Golden Record include photos of traffic jams in Thailand, construction sites in Africa (the country in Africa is not specified), a violin beside a music score, the parameters of the solar system, a nursing mother, an airplane in flight, and a page from Newton's System of the World, where that particular genius details the means of launching an object into orbit for the very first time.

Creating and curating an Instagram account can feel a little stupid. I sometimes wonder if I should be doing something in real life instead of online, and if this whole thing is a fool's errand. After all, is anyone even looking, and if they are, do they care? The team who made the Golden Record understood how tiny the chances were of any other life-form finding the craft, and then the record, and knowing how to decipher what they found there, and finally, understanding the message. That did not put the team off; they threw themselves into the effort, curating a collection of sounds, from a kiss to a night chant by Navajos to the brain waves of a woman in love.

That woman's name is Ann Druyan, and she was the creative director of the Golden Record. It was her idea to measure the electrical impulses of a human brain and nervous system, turn it into sound, and put it on the record. *Smithsonian* magazine reported on how this came to be, drawing from *Murmurs of Earth*, the book about the Golden Record. In an hour-long session hooked to an EEG at New York University Medical Center, Druyan meditated on a series of prepared thoughts. In *Murmurs of Earth* she admits that "a couple of irrepressible facts of my own life" slipped in. She and Carl Sagan had gotten engaged just days before, so a love story may very well be documented in her neurological signs. Compressed into a minute-long segment, the brain waves sound, writes Druyan, like a "string of exploding firecrackers." Thousands of years from now, as the spacecraft continue to spin through the cosmos, an alien civilization may find and decipher that data, turning it back into thoughts. They will read her mind, and know how she felt on that day long ago on a planet far away.

It's strangely moving to look at all the images too. One photo cracks me up—three people in unmistakably 1970s outfits, a woman licking an ice-cream cone with her tongue very far out, a man biting into a toasted cheese sandwich, and another man pouring water into his mouth from a jug he is holding over his head. It's so that the aliens can see how we lick, bite, and drink. It is surely far-fetched to think that this will help in the great quest to communicate ourselves in any way. As Carl Sagan noted, "The spacecraft will be encountered and the record played only if there are advanced spacefaring civilizations in interstellar space." The chances are tiny, and it hasn't happened yet, as the *Voyagers* travel farther and farther away from their home planet. He continues, "But the launching of this bottle into the cosmic ocean says something very hopeful about life on this planet." So you see, it's essential to try.

Today, with these images I get to share with anyone who cares to look, I am asking the question: *Do you understand me now? Here is what I'm trying to tell you.* Back home in Ireland I'm trying so hard, I feel quite desperate. *Look, I'll show you. This is the slurry tank I grew up beside. It is big and navy blue and has the word* HOWARD *stamped on its rounded sides. Do you know now that often I and my five sisters would have to fly through the house closing all the windows because Howard was acting up? Okay, good. So next I need you to look at these people sitting on a wall, they're watching a hurling game, okay? I didn't play and I still feel awkward when taxi drivers start slagging me over a Cork team I know nothing about. After the hurling pitch we drive past the graveyard, that's where my four grandparents are, I wish you could know them. My grandfather was a writer too but he didn't get very far. I miss him, actually. This is my lunch, I ordered too much because I'm not doing well, got it? Here's a terrible word joke where I collate quiche/capisce—I can't help thinking of puns because that's the way my brain works—are we clear? Here is me dancing alone in my room, I would never have shown you this a year ago, why now? I'm quite lonely today.*

In the digital world, Twitter is the murky ocean full of snapping things, Facebook is the endless landmass, our own patches well trodden, the rest full of impassable borders. When we're online, wandering around, we can run into any and all kinds of horror, but not on Instagram. It's the sky, clear and pretty. We must reach up toward it, we can only hope to flit through it, feeling light-headed from all of those aspirational aches. It isn't quite real, crammed with the pretty parts of life, the sunrises and laughing friends and roses in bloom. We censor the ugliness, you won't often hear a cruel word there, or see a fight, or have to reckon with some hurt you've caused. I'm fine with that. The Golden Record does not include the sound of gunshots or screams of pain; there were no images of war or cruelty included, only of creativity and beauty. We presented what was best about us. Sanitized, yes, fully honest, no, but there is a value in that too. That is our best selves, the choices we wish to make, the future we long to have. This is me, and this is my home. There it is, in a picture. We cannot say we are lost, we need only look up into space, or down at our phones, to see where we need to go, to remind ourselves of the way home.

Sources and Acknowledgments

Most of this book is memoir and some of it is reported and researched, so I'll list my sources here. There is a great piece in *New York* magazine, by Jesse Green, about the "other" Annie Moore, and how the confusion around Annie's identity was solved. Megan Smolenyak Smolenyak was instrumental to this story and is a tireless "genie" and a wonderful caretaker of Annie's legacy. On the other side of the Atlantic, back in Cobh, local historian Michael Martin provided me with valuable insight into what Annie was leaving behind. The Cobh Heritage Centre is full of wonderful resources for anyone hoping to find out more about emigration from Ireland.

Thanks also to my guide Brendan Murphy and all the staff of the Tenement Museum and to Barry Moreno, historian at the Ellis Island Immigration Museum, for their kindness and incredible work at uncovering and preserving this crucial part of the American story. To learn more about the history of U.S. immigration laws, have a read of Kunal M. Parker's *Making Foreigners: Immigration and Citizenship Law in America, 1600–2000*. To learn more about the time Frederick Douglass spent in Ireland, I read a wonderful account by Tom Chaffin, published in *The New York Times* in 2011, titled "Frederick Douglass's Irish Liberty." As mentioned in the essay, there is a fascinating paper by Lee Jenkins titled "Beyond the Pale: Frederick Douglass in Cork," published in *The Irish Review*, that details and contextualizes the trip further. To read Douglass's own account of that time in his life, which is stunning, read the second volume of his autobiography, titled *My Bondage and My Freedom*.

The writer Rachel Kaadzi Ghansah's unparalleled coverage of Dylann Roof in *GQ* magazine helped me to better understand the legacy of white supremacy in the U.S. *The Crossing* is essential viewing for anyone trying to understand the migrant crisis; it's an RTÉ documentary that follows the crew of the LÉ *Samuel Beckett* during their life-saving mission in the Mediterranean during the deadly summer of 2016.

I first heard of Friendship Park through some brilliant reporting done by Esther Yu Hsi Lee for *Think-*

Progress and Griselda San Martin for *The New York Times*. I am grateful to Dan Watman of Friends of Friendship Park for taking me there, and to Enrique Morones for his insight and his work with Border Angels. I highly recommend *Violent Borders: Refugees and the Right to Move* by Reece Jones, detailing how various governments attempt to contain populations and control access to resources and opportunities. Thank you to Liana and Vlad Ghica for allowing me into their lives. Huge gratitude is due to the immigrants I met and interviewed in the past couple of years. I am consistently impressed by the people I meet who have come here to make their lives anew, arriving as asylum seekers or tech entrepreneurs, and I feel incredibly lucky to hear and share their stories.

To better understand the stunning story behind the *Voyager* mission, I recommend *The Farthest*, a documentary by the Irish director Emer Reynolds, featuring an interview with interplanetary scientist Carolyn Porco. Carolyn worked on the *Voyager* mission and I was fortunate enough to discuss it with her on the *StarTalk* podcast. Many thanks to her, to Neil deGrasse Tyson, and to all the scientists and producers in the *StarTalk* family for making me more cosmically conscious! Carl Sagan's book *Murmurs of Earth: The* Voyager *Interstellar Record* is a must-read if you want to know more about the process of making the Golden Record.

I first heard about the Syrian cartoonist Ali Ferzat in a feature on his work that appeared in *The Guardian* in 2013, by David Stelfox. A great resource for anyone getting into comedy is Joe Randazzo's book *Funny on Purpose: The Definitive Guide to an Unpredictable Career in Comedy*. The Margaret Atwood quote that appears in "How Funny" is from *Second Words: Selected Critical Prose, 1960–1982*.

Most of this book is new work, but I've used some writing that has previously appeared in my other books and columns as the starting point for new pieces. Many thanks to my songbird editor at Hachette, Ciara Considine, for her work on what would become "Rent the Runway" and "Swimming Against Dolphins" and "Call Me Maeve." For that last one, I found a fun website called queenmaeve.org that had some new mythology and information (to me, at least) about my name twin. Thanks to the great Roisin Ingle at *The Irish Times* for commissioning me to cover Saint Patrick's Day in New York. Rachel Dry at *The New York Times* provided me with inspiration, brilliant editing, and, importantly, deadlines, for columns that eventually became "Summer Isn't the Same Without You" and "Aliens of Extraordinary Ability."

I would be lost without my literary agent Lindsay Edgecombe and our stoop meetings and emergency calls. This book would not exist without her. My editor,

Sarah Stein, shocked me with her generosity—with time, encouragement, and ideas—thanks to these two women, I did not feel alone all the time.

I also listened to Frank Ocean's album "Blonde" on repeat throughout and I will always love you how I do.

I'm grateful to the entire team at Penguin for their creativity, patience, and hard work, including Dave Cole, Matt Vee, Brianna Linden, Rebecca Marsh, Allison Carney, and especially Shannon Kelly.

Many thanks and much love to the following people who did all sorts of things to help me along the way: Philip Lyons, Tim McGabhann, Mel Glenn, Faith O'Grady, Shaina Feinberg, Erika Romero, Matt Shilts, Jim Hamblin, Julie Smith Clem, Naomi Westwater Weekes, Mona Chalabi, Emma Lee Moss, Chenoa Estrada, and all my darling book club sluts, including you, Jack!

My biggest thanks must go to my family for putting up with me and understanding me; to my parents and brother and sisters, and my sister- and brothers-in-law, and to all of my nieces and nephews, who brighten every day and to whom this book is dedicated. How I got to be so lucky, I will never know!